Joe Swash is a much-loved television presenter, broadcaster and actor, best known for playing Mickey Miller in *EastEnders*, as well as presenting *I'm a Celebrity: Extra Camp* for ITV2 and winning *Dancing on Ice* 2020. He was crowned King of the Jungle on *I'm a Celebrity... Get Me Out of Here!* in 2008. Joe is also a regular guest presenter on *Loose Women* and *Good Morning Britain*, covering entertainment and competitions. Most recently, Joe voiced the character of Sonny in *Thomas & Friends: Marvellous Machinery* and was a finalist in *Celebrity MasterChef* on BBC One.

Joe's Kitchen

Joe's Kitchen

Homemade meals
for a happy family

JOE SWASH

PAVILION

CONTENTS

Food for a happy family

My happy place is the dinner table. I have such great memories from when I was a kid, of sitting round the table with my mum and dad and my sisters, talking, laughing and taking the mick out of each other. The food may have only been something simple like sausages and mash, but it was good, and meals were a time we were all together, sometimes squabbling and arguing, but together and that's what mattered. Then we'd fight about who was going to do the washing up! Looking back, I realize I didn't appreciate just how important those moments were at the time. I wish I had.

This is something so close to my heart. Thanks to the amazing women in my life when I was growing up, women who fed and nourished me and made me who I am, I know the importance of making and sharing good food. I'm loving passing this on to my own kids, and I want to help you do the same.

What I've learned is that cooking and meal times are not just about eating – they're about sharing love, having quality time. Now I have my own family, I've realized just how vital and precious that is. I love food but more than anything I like seeing my family enjoying what I've cooked. For me, cooking is a sort of therapy – I enjoy it and I find it satisfying. I want to give you some insight into my life and my experiences in the kitchen. My food isn't fancy but it's good stuff and my family love it.

I had a great start. My mum was – and still is – a good cook and she was passionate about cooking my dad's favourite dishes and making him happy. They loved each other so much and for her, cooking was a way of showing that love. We didn't have a lot of money, but she would always produce great food on a low budget.

My dad was a London black cab driver and he liked to cook too – looking back I realize that he was a really modern man. Breakfast was his speciality. He loved a poached egg, and he was health conscious. He would cut all the fat off his bacon, then Mum would eat it! He enjoyed all the British classics like a Sunday roast, his mum's pies and stews, and his own signature dish was toad in the hole. He was a great family man, but he died very suddenly when I was 11

and life changed. Dramatically. For the next few years, we were so deep in grief that sitting round the dinner table together didn't feel right any more. The feeling of safety and security Dad brought to our family had gone, and I missed him so much. I spent years grieving and it was a long time before I felt normal again. All I wanted was to bring back that feeling of safety and happiness. And by the time the clouds had parted a bit we were teenagers, busy going out with our friends, and those family moments round the table remained a thing of the past.

Now, though, those wonderful memories from when my dad was alive have given me the best foundation both for how to be a dad and the family cook. Stacey's from much the same background as me, and food, family and togetherness are hugely important to her, like they are for me. I like to do most of the cooking in our house and I've had to up my game now I'm with her. She's more health conscious than I used to be and of course we both want our kids to have healthy, nourishing food. I've got better at trimming the fat off meat and using things like kale and coconut oil, stuff I wouldn't have tried before. I make more salads and get as much veg as possible into family meals.

Life is hectic with five kids in the house and when we're all back home after work and school it's chaos, I can tell you! Everyone is busy doing their own thing – homework, stuff on the computer, phones going and so on. When I call them for dinner, they might groan and protest – there might be shouts of 'Can I have one more game?', but we insist they come and sit down at the table.

Once they do, it's like the calm after the storm, a moment of clarity and peace in the day. And though they probably wouldn't admit it, they do enjoy meal times – that time to talk, share the day. It's so important, not just for the food but for the family relationships. It's proper quality time like I used to have with my mum and dad and sisters, and we take pride and pleasure in providing it. We also find it's a great time for getting the kids – particularly the teenagers – to open up and talk about what's going on in their lives. When we're all round the table and busy eating they drop their guard a bit and we get to hear about things we might not otherwise.

A game changer for me came in 2021 when I was asked to take part in *Celebrity MasterChef*. Me! On a cooking programme! I didn't expect to last five minutes, but I loved every minute of it, and I even made the finals. They all said I was the messiest cook they'd ever seen – this is a massive bugbear for Stacey as well! – but I did OK, and I was proud of myself. It really helped me take my cooking to another level and want to cook better and better food. I might have been messy, but some say that all the best creative people are messy. At least, that's what I tell myself!

Cooking has become a real passion and *MasterChef* made me realize that some dishes that seemed unachievable were actually simple. I didn't have much time to practise so I just had to rock in there and get on with it and I found it helped me find my own identity as a cook and gave me confidence. I loved working with all those chefs – people like Tom Kerridge. They were amazing teachers and taught me so much about timing and how to work in stages to build a great meal.

I learned all sorts of things, like what sort of oil to use when, how to make triple-cooked chips (mine are the best!) and I can even cook a soufflé. I never thought I would be able to do anything like that, but it's not hard once you know how. And I've discovered that once you've mastered the basics of something like a soufflé, you can make different flavours.

Now it's back to cooking for the family and I'm loving it. It's a real passion. The kids are good eaters on the whole. There are things they don't like, but I'm learning ways of getting them to eat stuff they might turn their noses up at. For instance, the boys used to say they didn't like broccoli but if I put a dash of teriyaki sauce on it, they'll eat it happily. I try to get the kids involved and find if they've helped make something, they're more likely to eat it. When I was a kid, Mum and Dad insisted on us doing the washing up and drying. But my lot – not a chance! I hope that giving my children this experience of family meal times – the experience I had as a kid of feeling protected and loved – will inspire them to do the same with their families down the line. And maybe I can inspire you too. By trial and error, I've come up with my own ways of making great meals for my family. The recipes in my book are for people like me – people with busy lives who want to do the best for those they love. I want to tell you what works for me and the tips and hacks I've been lucky enough to pick up over the years. I've learned a lot and I know that I can provide good, tasty meals for my family without complicated techniques or expensive ingredients. This is family-friendly food that you want to eat and is easy to achieve. Hope you love it all too.

Joe's Tips ♡

I love my potato peeler – it's one of my favourite kitchen tools and it's not just for peeling spuds. I use it for lots of things, like making nice thin slices of cheese and cucumber for sandwiches. And when I'm cooking for little Rex, I cut thin slivers of carrot as they cook so quickly – and he likes them that way.

When I'm making gravy – from scratch or from granules – I often use water from cooking the veg to add extra flavour. I add a knob of butter, too, to give the gravy a lovely shine.

I have to admit I can be a bit heavy-handed with the salt sometimes and that can ruin a good dish. If I realize I've chucked too much into something like a soup or a gravy, I add a wedge of potato or apple, then simmer for 10 minutes. The potato or apple soaks up the salt nicely and makes everything OK again.

If you need softened butter for baking or spreading and it's come cold out of the fridge or freezer, don't despair. I grate it on the coarse side of a grater and it's then fine to use.

When I'm cooking pasta, I often add a tablespoon of olive oil to the water – it stops the pasta sticking together. ♡

Vegetable scraps like onion skins, leek tops, carrot peelings, pea pods and mushroom trimmings can be used in veg stock. Just make sure they are clean and not browning or yellowing and store them in a bag in the freezer until you have enough for stock – see my recipe on page 269. But don't use potato peelings as they are too starchy, or anything from the cabbage family as they start to smell a bit too strong when simmered for a long time.

Add a lemon wedge or some lemon juice to rice to stop it going sticky. ♡

I love garlic but I don't like peeling it and I don't like having garlicky hands. So I quickly separate the cloves, then pop them in jam jar with a lid and give them a good shake. Most of the papery skins fall off – and your fingers won't be so smelly!

I always used to cry like a baby when peeling onions, but someone told me to put a teaspoon in my mouth. And you know what? It works.

I've discovered that a pizza cutter works really well for chopping herbs.

I used to be a messy cook, but now I'm much better at keeping tidy. I hang a compostable/biodegradable food waste bag on a cupboard door near where I'm working, or put a bowl on the work surface, and chuck any debris in there.

We like making cakes in our house and to speed things up, I prepare big jars of the basic ingredients. So I might have a Madeira cake jar, with all the flour and sugar measured out, or a crumble jar with all the flour, oats and sugar that's needed. That way, you just have to add the eggs and other wet ingredients and the whole process is much quicker.

Look out for these symbols on the recipes

QUICK — 30 minutes or less

ONE-POT — only needs one pot, pan, tin or tray

FREEZE — suitable for freezing

BREAKFAST
and
BRUNCH

Get the day off to a tasty start

Weekday mornings are chaotic for us – getting everyone up and dressed and off to nursery, school or work. But at weekends and days off when we can take our time, we like to make something a bit special. I love eggs, so a full English or eggs Benedict are favourites, and the kids go crazy for dishes like French toast and American pancakes.

QUICK

Sausage *and* Egg Muffins

These make a great treat for a weekend breakfast or brunch. It is worth making the sausages into patties like this – they cook quicker, and they make a neater little package to eat. Chef rings might sound a bit fiddly, but actually they are really useful and make it easy to get your patties and fried eggs just the right size.

Serves 4

250g sausage meat (about 5 fat sausages, squeezed from the skins)
1 small shallot or onion, very finely chopped
2 tsp dried (rubbed) sage
1 tsp garlic powder
plain flour, for dusting
olive or vegetable oil and butter, for frying
4 slices of cheese (optional)
4 eggs
4 pinches of dried sage or oregano
4 muffins, split and lightly toasted
ketchup, brown sauce or your favourite condiment

1. First make the sausage patties. Put the sausage meat, shallot or onion, sage and garlic powder into a bowl and mix thoroughly. Divide the mixture into 4 pieces.

2. Dust a work surface with flour. Put a chef ring on the floured surface and drop one of the pieces of sausage meat into it. Dust the top of the sausage meat with flour and press it out evenly into a flat patty, filling the ring. Repeat with the other 3 pieces of sausage meat.

3. Heat some oil in a frying pan. Take the sausage patties out of the rings and fry them over a medium heat until well browned and cooked through. This should only take around 2–3 minutes on each side. If using cheese, place a slice on each patty when you have flipped them. Putting a lid on the pan will help the cheese melt.

4. Heat some butter in another frying pan. Grease 4 chef rings with a little oil. Place them on the pan, break an egg into each one and sprinkle over a pinch of sage or oregano. Cover the pan with a lid and cook until the whites are set.

5. Pile the sausage patties and eggs into the muffins with your choice of condiment and serve immediately.

Joe's Tip

If I'm adding cheese to these, I find it's easier to use 2 frying pans so the cheese slices can be melting at the same time as I'm frying the eggs. Without the cheese, the sausage patties can be fried first – they will keep hot stacked to one side in the frying pan while the eggs are cooking in the same pan.

Full English *with* Hash Browns

I'm half Irish and, like all my family, I can't seem to have a meal without some sort of potato. I love them with everything – a plate isn't complete without them. So, hash browns are a definite winner for me with a full English breakfast.

Serves 4

4–8 sausages
olive oil
4–8 slices of bacon
4 slices of black pudding
400g chestnut or small
  portobello mushrooms, halved
4 medium tomatoes, halved
a few drops of balsamic vinegar
½ tsp dried oregano
15g butter
2 tbsp olive oil
2 slices of bread, cut in half
  diagonally
4–8 eggs
salt and black pepper

HASH BROWNS
400g floury potatoes, such as
  Maris Pipers or King Edwards,
  unpeeled and coarsely grated
1 medium onion, very finely
  chopped
½ tsp dried thyme
oil and butter, for frying

1. Preheat your oven to 200°C/180°C fan/gas 6. Put the sausages in a large roasting tin and drizzle them with 1 tablespoon of olive oil. Roast in the oven for 20 minutes until starting to brown all over. Give the tin a shake every so often.

2. Add the bacon, black pudding and mushrooms to the tin. Sprinkle the mushrooms with salt. Add the tomatoes and drizzle a few drops of balsamic vinegar over each cut half. Sprinkle with the oregano. Drizzle everything with another tablespoon of olive oil.

3. Roast in the oven for another 10–15 minutes, until the tomatoes are soft and everything is cooked through. Flip the slices of black pudding over once during this time.

4. While everything is roasting in the oven, cook the hash browns. Put the grated potato in the middle of a clean tea towel. Bring the sides up and squeeze to get rid of as much liquid as possible. Add the onion and sprinkle with 1 teaspoon of salt. Leave to stand for 5 minutes and squeeze again – the salt helps draw out more liquid. Add more salt, along with the thyme and plenty of black pepper.

5. Heat 2 tablespoons of olive oil in a frying pan. Butter 4 chef rings generously and divide the potato mixture between them, packing it down so it sticks together. Fry over a medium heat for several minutes, then flip – the hash browns should just drop back to the bottom of the ring onto the base of the frying pan but help them along if they stick. Cook for another 3–4 minutes until crisp and golden on the underside.

6. Remove the hash browns from the pan and keep warm. Add the olive oil to the same pan and fry the bread, turning until glossy and golden brown on both sides. Melt a knob of butter in a separate frying pan and fry the eggs, then serve at once.

Joe's Tip

I sometimes like to finish this in individual pans – add a small knob of butter to 4 pans. When it has melted, divide the contents of the roasting tin between the pans and add a hash brown. Break 1–2 eggs into each pan and cook until the whites are set, then slide onto warmed plates. Fry the bread separately or serve with toast.

Veggie Frittata

This is the Italian version of the omelette and contains a real feast of vegetables. I've suggested my favourite combo, but you can choose what you like and it's a good way of using up bits and bobs from the fridge. Great hot from the pan but you can also cut your frittata into wedges and eat it cold as a packed lunch or for a picnic.

Serves 4

300g potatoes, unpeeled, cut into chunks

200g tenderstem broccoli

100g peas (fresh or frozen)

1 tbsp olive oil

6 spring onions, cut into 3cm lengths

2 garlic cloves, finely chopped

15g butter

6 eggs

1 tsp dried mint

100g feta

a few fresh mint or basil leaves

salt and black pepper

1. Put the potatoes in a saucepan and add enough water to cover. Add 1 teaspoon of salt. Bring to the boil and simmer for about 10 minutes – the potatoes should be almost cooked through.

2. Add the broccoli to the same pan and simmer until just tender – another 2–3 minutes. Add the peas for the final minute. Drain thoroughly and set aside. Preheat your grill to a medium–high heat.

3. Heat the olive oil in a frying pan. Add the spring onions and cook over a medium heat until starting to brown. Add the garlic and cook for another minute, then add the butter.

4. Add all the vegetables to the pan and stir a couple of times so they take on some of the garlicky butter.

5. Beat the eggs with the dried mint and season with salt and pepper, then pour them into the pan around the vegetables. Put the feta on top (it should sink into the liquid egg) and shred the mint or basil leaves and sprinkle over.

6. Cook until completely set underneath – if you carefully prise up the edge it should be a rich golden brown. When the egg is almost set through, place the pan under the grill to finish it off. It may puff up a little, but this will recede as it cools.

7. Leave the frittata to cool for a few minutes before attempting to remove it from the pan. Cut into wedges and serve.

Joe's Tip

These can also be made in large 4-hole Yorkshire pudding tins. After frying the spring onions and garlic, add the vegetables and cook for a couple of minutes. Divide the mixture between the tins, add the eggs, feta and fresh and dried herbs, then bake in an oven preheated to 200°C/180°C fan/gas 6 for 12–15 minutes.

Classic French Omelette

A classic omelette is simple and quick to make but you need to get the technique right. I've got the knack now and I know that it's really important to get all the bits and pieces prepped and ready to go before you start cooking. Make sure your pan is good and hot before you add the butter, then follow the method below and you should be fine.

Serves 1

BASIC OMELETTE
3 eggs, beaten
½ tsp dried oregano or
   mixed dried herbs
large knob of butter
salt and black pepper

FILLING
25g ham, diced
25g hard cheese, such
   as Cheddar, Gruyère
   or Gouda, grated

OPTIONAL EXTRAS
1 tbsp onion, very finely chopped
1 medium tomato, very finely
   chopped
50g spinach, wilted in a pan,
   squeezed of liquid and
   chopped
1 sprig of tarragon, leaves
   finely chopped
a few chives, finely snipped

1. First get everything ready. Mix the ham and cheese together and add any of the optional extras you like.

2. Beat the eggs together with salt and pepper and the dried herbs.

3. Heat an omelette pan until it is nice and hot. Add the butter – it should immediately start melting and foaming. Swirl it around the pan until the whole base is coated.

4. Working very quickly, pour in the beaten egg mixture and swirl it round the base. Take a fork or palette knife and pull the set edges of omelette into the middle of the pan so that the uncooked eggs can fill the space. Keep doing this until there is no more egg left to fill the gaps. Leave to cook for another minute until it doesn't look wet on top.

5. Sprinkle the filling in a line down the middle, then carefully fold one side of the omelette over it. Fold over the other side, then flip it over until it is fold-side down. Slide onto a plate and eat immediately.

Eggs Benedict

This is one of my all-time favourite breakfasts, sometimes with a bit of ham or crunchy bacon alongside. An absolute treat in the morning. And have a go at my tip for cooking the eggs in advance so you can reheat them all together. It really works.

Serves 4

4–8 eggs (depending
  on appetite)
2 tbsp white wine vinegar
4 muffins, halved and toasted

BÉARNAISE SAUCE
1 shallot, very finely chopped
6 large sprigs of tarragon
  (see method)
a few black peppercorns
3 tbsp white wine vinegar
2 egg yolks
200g butter, softened
squeeze of lemon juice
  (optional)
salt and pepper

1. Start with the sauce. Put the shallot in a very small saucepan. Strip the leaves from the tarragon, finely chop them and set aside. Lightly bruise the stems and add them to the pan along with the peppercorns. Pour in the vinegar and add 1 tablespoon of water.

2. Bring to the boil, then turn the heat down and leave to simmer until the liquid has reduced to about 1 tablespoon. Strain and leave to cool.

3. Put the egg yolks in a small bowl with 1 tablespoon of water. Place the bowl over a pan of gently simmering water. Add the reduced vinegar and whisk until well combined. Add the butter a teaspoon at a time, whisking constantly. Make sure the butter emulsifies with the egg yolks each time before you add any more.

4. When you have added all the butter you should have a smooth, creamy yellow sauce. Stir in the chopped tarragon leaves and leave to stand for a minute, then taste. Add salt, pepper and a squeeze of lemon juice if you think the sauce needs it.

5. To keep the sauce warm, turn off the heat but leave the bowl sitting over the saucepan of water. Cover the bowl. Give the sauce another good whisk just before serving.

6. To poach the eggs so that they are all ready at the same time, part cook them first. This can be done a day in advance. Prepare a large bowl of iced water.

7. Bring a saucepan of water to the boil and add a generous pinch of salt and the white wine vinegar. Break an egg into a ramekin, then drop it into a fine mesh sieve. Swirl it around so that the excess white drops away – this will help stop your egg from looking straggly and give it a better shape once cooked.

Continued on the next page

8. Turn the heat down so the water is just simmering, then create a whirlpool effect by stirring vigorously in one direction. Drop the egg into the centre of it. Leave to cook for 1½–2 minutes until the white has formed together and firmed up. The yolk will still be runny. Remove the egg with a slotted spoon and drop into the iced water. Repeat with the remaining eggs. When they are cold, cover the bowl and put it in the fridge.

9. When you are ready to eat, toast the muffins and heat some water in a large pan. When the water is boiling, turn the heat down to a low simmer. Using a slotted spoon, carefully drop the eggs in. Cook for another minute until piping hot.

10. Serve the eggs on the muffins with the béarnaise sauce spooned over the top.

Joe's Tip

The sauce is easier than you think, but if it does split, here's what to do. Whisk in up to about 2 teaspoons of hot water, a few drops at time. If that doesn't work, start again with another egg yolk. Add the split sauce, a few drops at a time to start with, until it emulsifies, then pour it in very, very slowly and steadily until you have added it all. If the sauce then needs thinning, add a few more drops of water.

ONE-POT

Nanny Fran's Bubble *and* Squeak

My nanny Fran did a great bubble and squeak and I think her recipe had been passed down to her from her family. I hated it when I was a kid, but I've grown to love a good bubble and it's a great way of using up leftover mash and other veg – you can add anything you like. I use chef rings to make neat patties, but you can make one big bubble if you prefer.

Serves 4

400g cooked mashed potatoes
150g peas, defrosted
100g cooked sliced cabbage
200g cooked broccoli florets, roughly chopped
100g Cheddar, grated (optional)
1 tbsp wholegrain mustard
50g plain flour
olive oil or butter, for greasing and frying
salt and black pepper

1. Put the mashed potato into a bowl with the peas, cabbage, broccoli florets, cheese, if using, and mustard. Season generously with salt and pepper.

2. Divide the mixture into 4 portions. Shape them into patties and dust generously with flour. Lightly oil or butter 4 chef rings and press a patty into each one. Chill in the fridge for at least 30 minutes.

3. When you are ready to cook the patties, heat a frying pan and add just enough oil or butter to coat the base. Add the patties in their rings and cook until a crust has formed on the underside. Flip over and press down lightly to make sure the patty is in contact with the frying pan, then cook for another few minutes.

4. Serve as part of a breakfast or brunch, perhaps with bacon and eggs.

Joe's Tip

Prepare ahead tip – these are best cooked from chilled, so easy to make the day before and store in the fridge until you're ready to cook them.

QUICK

Breakfast Hash

My dad used to like a corned beef hash, but I prefer to make mine with plenty of veg and a bit of bacon or sausage. I use freshly cooked vegetables in this recipe, but you can also make hash with any leftover cooked vegetables, such as roast potatoes, plus some meat from the Sunday joint.

Serves 4

300g floury potatoes, such as
    Maris Pipers or King Edwards,
    unpeeled and diced
200g carrots, peeled and diced
200g celeriac, peeled and diced
200g cauliflower or broccoli
    florets, roughly chopped
2 tbsp olive oil
1 large onion, finely chopped
150g smoked bacon or chorizo or
    cooked meat, diced
leaves from 1 sprig of thyme
1 tsp Worcestershire sauce
1 tbsp brown sauce or ketchup
leftover gravy (optional)
salt and black pepper

OPTIONAL EXTRAS
fried eggs
chopped parsley

1. Put the potatoes, carrots and celeriac into a saucepan. Cover with water, bring to the boil and season with salt.

2. Cook for 3 minutes, then add the cauliflower or broccoli. Continue to cook for another 2 minutes, then drain.

3. Heat the olive oil in a large frying pan. Add the onion and cook over a medium–high heat until it looks translucent and is starting to brown. Add whichever meat you are using and fry until crisp.

4. Add all the cooked vegetables to the pan and stir to coat them with the oil. Add the thyme and season with salt and pepper. Fry over a high heat for 15–20 minutes, stirring every few minutes until crisp and well browned.

5. Stir in the Worcestershire sauce, the brown sauce or ketchup and any leftover gravy. Continue to cook until the sauces start to caramelize around the edges.

6. Serve on warm plates, top with fried eggs and scatter over some chopped parsley, if using.

My dad

Everything I've learned about being a parent I learned from my dad during the 11 years I had with him. He was a London black cab driver and the kindest, most fun and gentle man you could ever hope to meet.

He had friends everywhere – everyone loved my dad. I used to walk down the street in our old neighbourhood, and someone would come up and say, 'You're Ricky's boy?' and then tell me a story about something nice he'd done for them. He always supported me in whatever I wanted to do – like he'd take me to football training several times a week. He was my best friend as well as my dad and we did so much together. Money was tight but he always made sure we had great holidays. He bought a sort of trailer-caravan and every summer he'd hook it up to the car and we'd all drive off to the south of France and spend a month on a campsite by the beach. I have the most incredible memories of those times with my family.

Friday night was film night in our house, and one Friday we'd been watching Whoopi Goldberg in *Sister Act*. I remember Dad saying to me, 'Right, it's time for bed' and me arguing that I wanted to see some more. Next morning, I woke up to the most horrendous sound of Mum screaming. I ran to their bedroom and there she was, desperately trying to wake Dad up. I phoned 999 but I must have panicked and not explained properly, because they sent police, fire and ambulance – everything came. At one stage, my dad opened his eyes and looked at me, then he closed them again. That was the last time I saw him alive. Then he was taken away in the ambulance with Mum.

I went to a friend's house with my sisters, and we didn't know what was happening. It was terrible. One of my uncles came and took us to the hospital and there we were told my dad had died. I didn't know what to do with myself and I just ran out of the hospital. It was all a blur and really traumatic. My dad had always been so fit. He would run several times a week, do marathons, cut the fat off his meat, but he died of something called Sudden Adult Death Syndrome. No one really understands it, but it can be genetic. The doctors told us it could have happened at any time – he was a ticking time bomb.

Trying to get on with life after that was so hard. When you're used to someone being such a support, then they're not there any more, it's tough. We didn't have any money – my dad had life insurance, but it turned out to be a fraud – and Mum had to sell Dad's cab. It was all we had. About two years later I remember being up in the West End and seeing it drive past. It was so strange to see the cab without him in it. I still struggle with the grief. I don't think I've ever dealt with my dad's death properly.

Money was tight but my dad always made sure we had great holidays

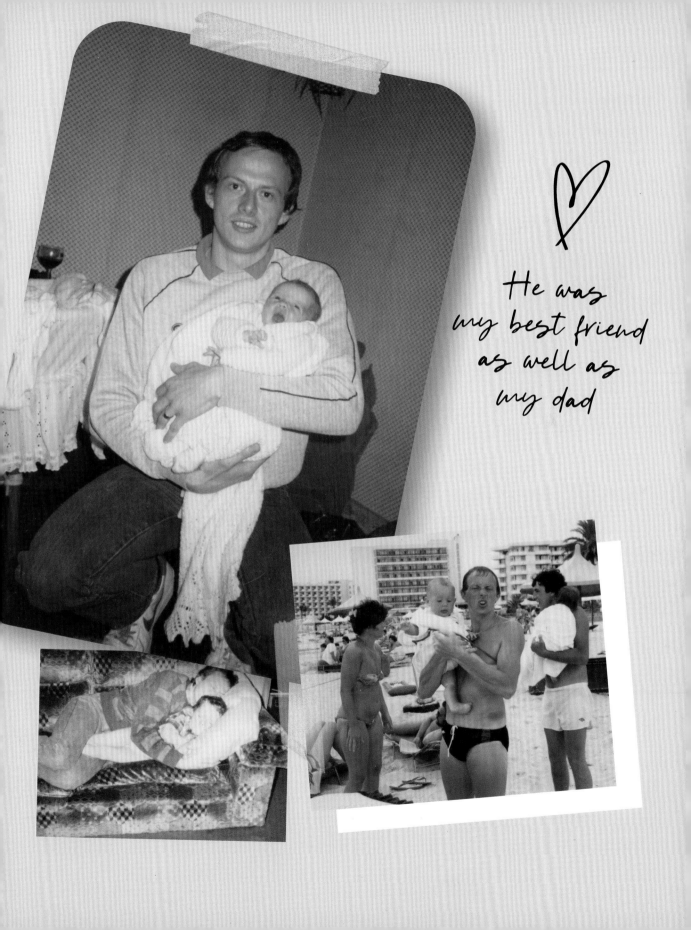

He was
my best friend
as well as
my dad

Savoury French Toast

My dad used to love smoked mackerel for breakfast. He was always first up – he was a London cab driver and liked to get out there early. He'd put this smoked peppered mackerel in the microwave and the smell would fill the house – not in a good way! I'm saving you all from that because the other thing he used to enjoy was savoury French toast and this recipe is a bit of a homage to him. My version is a sort of cross between a toastie and French toast and I promise you it smells much better than smoked mackerel first thing in the morning!

Makes 4

8 slices of bread
4 slices of ham
½ tsp dried oregano
75g mature Cheddar, grated
50g good melting cheese, such
  as block mozzarella
  or Gruyère, grated
ketchup, hot sauce or mustard
butter, for frying

EGG MIXTURE
6 eggs
150ml milk
½ tsp dried oregano
½ tsp garlic powder
pinch of hot chilli powder
salt and black pepper

1. Take 4 slices of the bread and top each one with a slice of ham. Sprinkle with oregano. Mix the Cheddar and mozzarella or similar together and divide between the sandwiches. Drizzle over some ketchup or any condiment you like, then top with the remaining slices of bread. Squish them together as much as possible.

2. Whisk the eggs and milk together, then add the oregano, garlic powder and chilli powder. Season with salt and pepper and whisk again.

3. Dip each sandwich into the egg mixture, making sure it is well coated.

4. Melt a knob of butter in a large frying pan. When it has foamed, add as many of the sandwiches as you can fit – you'll most likely have to cook them in two batches. Cook over a medium heat for a few minutes on each side until the bread is a rich brown and the cheese has melted. Cut in half and serve.

Joe's Tip

It's best not to cook these on too high a heat or the outsides may burn before the cheese has melted. If you like, you can cook them in a sandwich toaster instead of in a frying pan.

American Pancakes

Breakfast pancakes always remind me of my first family holiday with Stacey and the boys. She was pregnant – although we didn't know it at the time – and we went to LA for two weeks. Every morning we'd get the kids up and they'd be so excited for breakfast – a feast of beautiful pancakes and maple syrup at Mel's Diner. I like to make pancakes American-style at home now and everyone still loves them.

Makes 16

50g butter
1 carton of buttermilk
  (usually 284ml)
about 90ml milk
½ tsp vanilla extract
1 egg
225g plain flour
1 tsp baking powder
½ tsp bicarbonate of soda
25g caster sugar
pinch of salt

TO SERVE

maple syrup or honey
400g berries, such as
  blueberries, raspberries,
  chopped strawberries
thick yoghurt, whipped cream
  or crème fraîche

1. Melt the butter in a small saucepan. Pour the buttermilk into a jug and add enough milk to make it up to 375ml. Add all but 1 tablespoon of the melted butter and the vanilla extract and egg, then beat to combine.

2. Put the flour, baking powder, bicarbonate of soda and sugar in a mixing bowl with a pinch of salt. Gradually add the wet ingredients to the dry to make a smooth batter.

3. Heat a non-stick or cast-iron pan over a medium–high heat, then rub the base with some of the reserved butter. Ladle over rounds of the pancake batter – about 2 tablespoons for each one.

4. Cook until each pancake looks set on top – it should look slightly shiny, and bubbles will start to appear. Check carefully to see if the underside is a rich brown, then flip and cook until the other side is also golden brown. Keep these pancakes warm by wrapping them in a clean tea towel or foil as you use up the remaining batter – you should be able to make around 4 at a time.

5. Serve in a stack with maple syrup or honey, berries and spoonfuls of yoghurt, whipped cream or crème fraîche.

Joe's Tip

If you don't have any buttermilk, you can make something similar at home. Just stir a good tablespoon of lemon juice into 250–300ml whole milk. Set it aside for 10 minutes and it will thicken up nicely.

QUICK MEALS and SNACKS

I'm always hungry - keep those snacks coming

There are always people around at our house and they want food! The kids come home from school starving, and I've become an expert at rustling up snacks that are fun and reasonably healthy too. They've learned to love kale chips – they'll sit munching those instead of crisps – and everyone enjoys a yoghurt ice lolly on a hot day.

Croissant Pizzas

When I was a kid, we used to go to the south of France every summer for our holidays. We didn't have much money, but we'd tow a caravan down there – it took three days – and we'd stay for a month. Every morning, me and my sisters would battle over who was going to cycle to the bakery to get croissants for breakfast, so they always bring back happy memories of those times. I love to use them to make a totally delicious pizza-style snack for the kids.

Makes 4

2 croissants, cut in half
  horizontally
100g block mozzarella, shredded
a few slices of pepperoni
a few basil leaves
1 tbsp olive oil

SAUCE

4 tbsp tomato purée
1 tbsp olive oil
1 medium tomato, finely
  chopped
1 tsp dried oregano or mixed
  Italian herbs
1 small garlic clove, crushed
a few basil leaves, finely
  chopped
pinch of caster sugar (optional)
salt and black pepper

1. Preheat your oven to 200°C/180°C fan/gas 6.

2. Make the sauce by mixing all the ingredients together and seasoning with salt and pepper. You can add a pinch of sugar too if you like, but the basil acts as a good sweetener.

3. Divide the sauce between the 4 pieces of croissant and spread evenly right to the edges. Top with the cheese and pepperoni. Tear up the basil leaves and scatter them over, then drizzle or brush over the oil.

4. Bake in the oven for about 10 minutes until the cheese has melted and everything has started to brown. Serve at once.

Scotch Eggs

When we used to go off to the south of France in our caravan for the summer holidays, my mum would save money by making picnics to take to the beach. There'd always be corned beef sandwiches – and I remember there would literally be sand in them as it gets everywhere when you eat on the beach! Scotch eggs were another regular and I loved them. I make them now with a bit of black pudding as well as sausage, and I add a little apple for extra flavour.

Makes 4

4 eggs
200g sausage meat
75g black pudding
1 small apple or ½ large apple
vegetable oil, for frying

COATING

50g plain flour
2 eggs
75g fine dry breadcrumbs
   or panko breadcrumbs
salt and black pepper

Joe's Tip

You can make nice little Scotch eggs with quails' eggs. The coating mix above is enough for 12 of them. Just part-cook the eggs for 1 minute, then follow the main recipe. You'll need about 25g of the sausage mixture for each egg.

1. First, part-cook the eggs. Put them in a saucepan and cover them with water. Bring to the boil and cook for 5 minutes. Remove from the heat and plunge the eggs into cold water to stop them from cooking any more, then peel them and set aside.

2. Break up the sausage meat and black pudding. Grate the apple onto some kitchen paper or a tea towel, then wrap it up and squeeze out as much of the liquid as you can. Add this to the sausage meat and black pudding and mix thoroughly.

3. Divide the mixture into 4 portions. Flatten each piece in your hand, then mould it around an egg. Bring the joins together by gently massaging until the whole egg is covered.

4. Put the flour, one of the eggs and half the breadcrumbs into 3 separate shallow bowls. Beat the egg thoroughly and season the flour with salt and pepper. Dip each Scotch egg into the flour, then the beaten egg and finally the breadcrumbs. Once you've coated two Scotch eggs, add the remaining egg and breadcrumbs to the bowls. That way things don't get too messy.

5. Pour the oil into a deep-fryer or a large saucepan, making sure the pan is no more than half full. Heat to 180°C. If you don't have a thermometer, test by adding a cube of bread – it should turn golden brown in 30 seconds if the oil is hot enough. Be very careful and never leave a pan of hot oil unattended.

6. Carefully lower two of the eggs into the oil and cook for 3–4 minutes until they turn a deep golden brown. Remove with a slotted spoon and place them on kitchen paper to drain. Repeat with the remaining eggs – it's best not to crowd your fryer or saucepan.

Cheese *and* Marmite Scrolls

Australia and *I'm a Celebrity...* mean so much to Stacey and me. We both won the Jungle, we met there, and we fell in love there – then we had our children, got married and our lives changed for ever. When we were presenting the spin-off show we'd go to the studio every Thursday morning and they'd have these cheese and Vegemite scrolls for breakfast. Stacey absolutely loved them and now we make them for the kids. They're special and when we eat these, we always get a little smile on our faces, as we remember those times Down Under.

Makes 12

DOUGH

500g strong white flour, plus extra for dusting
7g instant yeast
30ml olive oil
1 tsp Marmite
1 tsp salt
1 tsp sugar or honey
300ml tepid water

FILLING

2 tsp Marmite
30g cream cheese
75g Cheddar, grated

TOPPING

1 egg, beaten, for brushing
50g Cheddar, grated

1. Put the flour and yeast in a bowl and stir. Drizzle in the oil, then add the Marmite, salt and sugar or honey. Gradually work in the water until you have a fairly sticky dough.

2. Turn the dough out onto a floured work surface and knead until it is smooth and elastic. There is a very simple test called the 'window pane test' to check if it has been kneaded for long enough. Very gently stretch the dough – if you can stretch it to the point where it is almost thin enough to see through, without it breaking, it is ready.

3. Put the dough back in the bowl and cover with a damp tea towel. Leave it somewhere warm for 1½–2 hours until it has puffed up to about twice the size.

4. Turn the dough onto a floured surface and knock the air out of it so it deflates. Shape it into a large rectangle – about 35 x 25cm. Mix the Marmite with the cream cheese – it will go quite runny – and spread it all over the bread. Sprinkle with the grated cheese.

5. Roll up the dough along the longest side, quite tightly, then cut it into 12 rounds. Arrange the rounds over a baking tray lined with baking paper. Space them a couple of centimetres apart as they will spread and touch one another – like a tear and share bread.

6. Cover with a damp tea towel and leave again – this time for about 30 minutes – until the dough has increased in size but is still quite firm. Preheat your oven to its highest setting.

7. Brush the rounds with beaten egg and sprinkle with cheese. Bake in the oven for 20–25 minutes until they are cooked through and a deep golden brown. Serve warm from the oven. Store any leftovers in an airtight tin for a few days.

Welsh Rarebit *with* Marmite

One of my dad's favourite snacks was Welsh rarebit, but I wasn't a fan as a kid. I thought it was Welsh rabbit and didn't want to eat it! Now, though, I'm addicted, and I have to stop myself eating them all day long – I'd end up being 20 stone! My special twist is to add a bit of Marmite for extra flavour, and I like a little very finely chopped onion too. Make sure to chop it really small though – you don't want to bite down on chunks of raw onion. The egg isn't essential, but it does make the rarebit nice and creamy.

Serves 4

250g hard cheese, such as
   Cheddar, grated
1 small onion, very finely
   chopped (optional)
1 tsp garlic powder
1 heaped tsp plain flour
15g butter
50ml beer or stout
1 tsp Worcestershire sauce
1 heaped tsp Marmite
1 egg, beaten
4 large slices of bread

1. Put all the ingredients, except the egg and the bread, in a saucepan and place it over a low–medium heat. Cook very gently, stirring or whisking regularly, until the cheese has melted. Be very careful not to let the mixture boil, as that will make the cheese split.

2. When the cheese has melted and the mixture is thick but still pourable, remove the pan from the heat and set aside for a few moments. Then whisk in the egg thoroughly, making sure it has properly combined with the rest of the ingredients.

3. Leave the mixture to cool until it is almost room temperature and has thickened up – you want to be able to spread it on the bread, not pour it.

4. Preheat the grill to a medium heat. Lightly toast the bread on both sides, then thickly spread the cheese mixture on top of each slice. Grill for a few minutes until the cheese has lightly browned.

Joe's Tip

The Marmite flavour is nicely subtle here, but if you're a big Marmite fan, spread some on one side of the toast before adding the cheese mixture to give an extra savoury hit.

My mum

KIP & JOE
x x

My mum is the most amazing, strong woman you could ever hope to meet. She was incredible after Dad died. She stepped up to the mark and she was our mum and our dad all wrapped up in one. She was only 35 and there she was on her own with three kids – my little sister was only two. She had no money, but she just got on with it.

My role in the family changed pretty dramatically too. I was the oldest, so I took on quite a bit of responsibility. My mum had some cleaning jobs in the evening as well as in the day, and I'd go with her because I didn't want her going out at night by herself. I was very protective of her – I think I was scared that something might happen to her too, and me and my sisters would be orphans.

Mum could have just given up after Dad died, but she never did. She used to say how disappointed he would be if he looked down and saw her letting everything go to pot. She worked her socks off for us, to keep us clothed and fed, and she did it all for him. I've never known anyone love someone as much as she loved my dad. She fought for us to have a good life. She even saved up money all year and learned to tow a caravan so she could take us on holiday to the south of France, like my dad always did. Thinking about it now, that was so incredible – her getting us all in the car, hitching up the caravan and driving three days through France. She was determined that we didn't miss out on anything.

I know I wouldn't be where I am now without Mum. Much later on when I was in my twenties and in a really dark place, she was such an amazing support. She always looked out for me. And she looked out for others too. Once we were all grown up, she became a foster carer. She looked after a little girl from six months until she was four when she moved to a permanent family. Then Mum started looking after Daniel. He was eight when he first came to her and now he's about to go to university. He's part of our family and we're all so proud of him.

We have such a strong bond – my mum and me and my sisters. She grieved so much for my dad – he was the love of her life and she never met or wanted anyone else. She used to say to us that our dad was the most special person in the world, and she didn't want to bring any other man into our lives. She wanted us to grow up with our dad's example, with what we'd learned from him.

My mum and my sisters mean the world to me. We might row like cats and dogs and call each other all the names under the sun, but five minutes later everything's back to normal. Mum has a heart of gold and would do anything for anyone. I speak to her every day and we're together several times a week at least. We're as close as ever and we always will be.

Mum could have just given up after Dad died, but she never did

My mum and my sisters mean the world to me ♡

Hummus, Three Ways

My mum used to eat hummus years ago, long before it was the massively popular thing it is now. My mates would come round and say, 'What's this?' – they'd never seen it before. She'd make a big batch and mix it with bit of yoghurt, then we'd eat tons of it with carrot sticks and crackers or crisps. Here's my basic recipe and a few ways of pepping it up. You could also add these extras to a tub of shop-bought hummus if you're short on time.

Serves 4

BASIC HUMMUS

1 x 400g tin chickpeas, drained
1 tbsp tahini
juice of ½ lemon
1 garlic clove, crushed
1 tbsp olive oil
salt and black pepper

ROAST CARROT HUMMUS

2 medium carrots, cut into batons
1 tbsp olive oil
½ tsp ground cumin
½ tsp honey
sesame seeds or za'atar, to garnish

ROAST RED PEPPER HUMMUS

2 roast red peppers from a jar
1 tbsp olive oil
1 tsp harissa paste (or more, to taste)
chilli flakes, to garnish

SPICED ONION HUMMUS

1 tbsp olive oil
2 small red onions, thinly sliced
1 tsp cumin seeds
½ tsp honey
¼ tsp ground turmeric
¼ tsp ground cinnamon

1. For the basic hummus, put the chickpeas, tahini, lemon juice and garlic in a food processor and season with salt and pepper. Process until broken down into a purée – you may need to add a couple of tablespoons of water to help it. Drizzle in the olive oil. Taste and adjust the seasoning and add a bit more lemon juice if it needs it.

2. For the carrot hummus, preheat the oven to 200°C/180°C fan/gas 6. Put the carrots in a roasting tin and drizzle over the olive oil. Sprinkle with salt and the cumin. Roast for 15 minutes, then remove from the oven, drizzle over the honey and continue to roast for another 5–10 minutes until the carrots are just cooked through and browned around the edges. Purée the carrots on their own, then add the basic hummus and purée again. Garnish with sesame seeds or za'atar.

3. For the roast red pepper hummus, purée the peppers on their own, then add the harissa and basic hummus and purée again. Garnish with a few chilli flakes.

4. For the spiced onion hummus, heat the olive oil in a frying pan. Add the onions and cook over a medium heat, stirring regularly until crisping up and browning. Add the cumin seeds and honey and season with salt and pepper. Cook for another few minutes. Remove from the frying pan. Put half in a food processor with the spices and purée, then purée again with the basic hummus. Garnish with the remaining onions.

5. Serve your hummus with pitta bread and raw veg sticks.

TO SERVE

toasted pitta bread
batons of carrot, pepper,
   cucumber, courgette,
   celery, chicory and sugar
   snap peas
whole tomatoes and/or
   radishes

Joe's Tip

If you prefer to roast your own peppers, preheat the oven to 200°C/180°C fan/gas 6. Halve the red peppers, discarding any seeds and trimming off any white membrane. Put the peppers in a roasting tin and drizzle with olive oil. Roast for about 25 minutes until the peppers have softened and the skin has started to brown. Remove from the oven and cover with a clean tea towel – this will help them steam until they are cool enough to handle and will make the skins easier to remove. Peel the peppers if you want to.

Spiced Onion
Hummus

Basic
Hummus

Roast
Carrot
Hummus

Roast
Red Pepper
Hummus

Quesadillas

My kids love a quesadilla, and they make a great snack to serve up when they have friends round. I've suggested some extras, but you could also add guacamole (see my recipe on page 215), soured cream, leftover veg – whatever you fancy. I do put some fresh coriander in my quesadillas but it's a herb some people love and some hate. For most, it has a lemony taste, but if you have a particular gene, this herb tastes like soap! I'm one of those people but I see it as my problem, not everyone else's.

Serves 4-6

REFRIED BEANS

1 tbsp olive oil
1 onion, finely chopped
1 red pepper, finely chopped (optional)
2 garlic cloves, finely chopped
1 tsp ground cumin
1 tsp dried oregano
1 tsp mild chilli powder or hot sauce
400g tin black, kidney or pinto beans, drained
salt and black pepper

TO ASSEMBLE

4–6 tortillas (depending on size)
100g sweetcorn kernels
125g Cheddar, grated

OPTIONAL EXTRAS

pickled jalapeños
chopped coriander
2 spring onions, finely sliced

1. First make the refried beans. Heat the oil in a frying pan and add the onion and red pepper, if using. Cook gently over a medium heat until the onion is translucent and both onion and pepper have softened, adding the garlic for the last couple of minutes. Stir in the cumin, oregano and chilli powder or sauce.

2. Add the beans and about 50ml of water and season with salt and pepper. Stir until the beans are heated through. Mash roughly in the pan and continue to cook until the beans come away cleanly from the base of the pan – they need to be quite dry.

3. To assemble, spread a couple of tablespoons of the refried beans over one half of each tortilla. Sprinkle with the sweetcorn, cheese and any of the optional extras, and fold in half. Repeat with the remaining tortillas.

4. Heat a frying pan. Cook the quesadillas over a medium heat for a few minutes on each side until the cheese has melted and the outside is lightly brown and crisp. Cut into wedges. The easiest way to do this without the mixture spilling out is with a pizza cutter.

QUICK

Sesame Kale Chips

Before I lived with Stacey, I wasn't that healthy in my cooking, but she's got me eating things like kale. At first, I'd turn my nose up, but now I like it. The kids love these as a sofa snack when they're watching TV. I'm happy, as they're a healthy option and a good alternative to popcorn, but they still have that nice snacky crunchy feel. If your family love them as much as mine, you could double up on the ingredients and cook another batch while they're tucking into the first lot. I sometimes add a pinch of Chinese five spice for a bit of extra flavour.

Serves 4

100g curly kale
1 tbsp light olive oil
1 tsp dark or light soy sauce
2 tsp sesame seeds

1. Preheat your oven to 180°C/160°C fan/gas 4. Wash and dry the kale thoroughly, then strip the leaves from the stems, particularly if they are thick and woody.

2. Put the leaves in a bowl with the oil and soy sauce and mix thoroughly with your hands. Massage the leaves a little as you mix – this softens them slightly, which helps them to crisp up in the oven.

3. When the leaves are completely coated with the oil and soy, spread them over a couple of baking trays, making sure they aren't too tightly packed together. Sprinkle with the sesame seeds.

4. Bake in the preheated oven for 6–10 minutes. The timing will depend on how thick the leaves are – the smaller, more delicate ones will brown in 6 minutes. So keep checking and remove as they become crunchy. Leave to cool, then serve immediately.

Joe's Tip

You can leave some of the slimmer stems in place if you like, but if you do, the leaves won't dry out completely. If you want to keep the kale chips for more than a day, make sure you remove all the stems. No need to waste them – chop them up and add them to soups or stews at the same time as onions, celery or root veg.

Yoghurt Ice lollies

These are a Stacey thing and a really quick and easy way of giving the kids a treat, but a healthy treat. Some of the bought stuff is packed with additives and the kids are bouncing off the walls after eating them. So, whenever we can we keep things homemade and a bit healthier. Little Rex loves these and ends up with melting yoghurt all over his face!

Makes 12

400g Greek yoghurt
3 tbsp runny honey
200g berries, such as
   strawberries, blueberries,
   raspberries
squeeze of lemon or lime juice

1. Put the Greek yoghurt in a bowl and drizzle in the honey. Whisk very lightly so the honey is evenly distributed through the yoghurt.

2. Put the berries in a small bowl and crush them very lightly – you want a mixture of whole and broken up berries. Squeeze the lemon or lime juice over them.

3. Divide the yoghurt between twelve 50ml ice-lolly moulds. Spoon the fruit on top, then carefully stir each one so you get a ripple effect through each lolly. Add the lolly holders or sticks.

4. Put the lollies in the freezer and freeze until solid. They'll take least 3 hours but it's better to leave them overnight.

5. Remove the lollies from the freezer just before serving and let them stand for a few minutes to make them easier to remove from the moulds. Alternatively, dip the moulds very briefly in hot water.

Joe's Tip

If you don't have lolly moulds, you can make these in ice-cube trays.

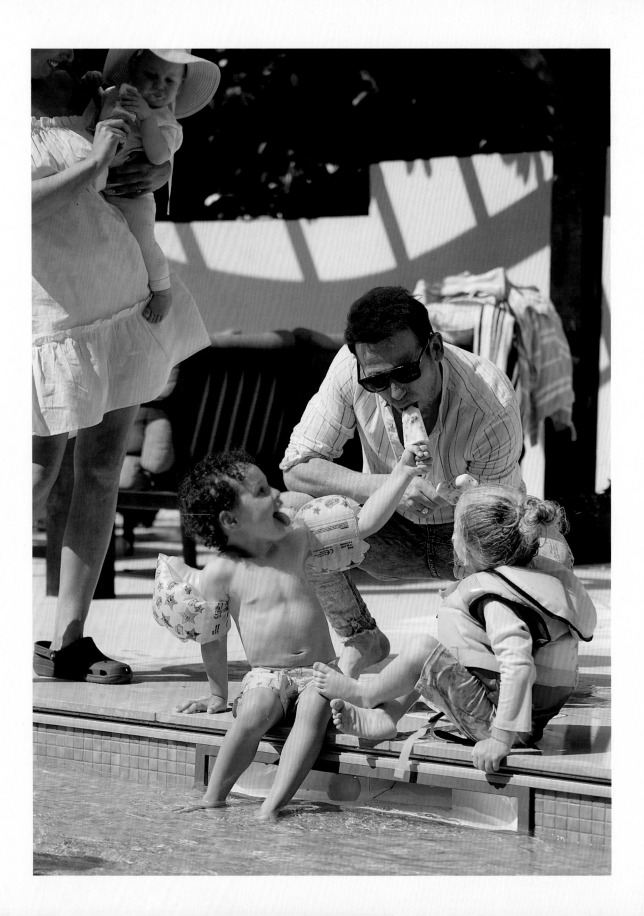

Fruity Flapjacks

I like to make these for a nice little treat for the kids when they've been racing round in the garden all afternoon. They are sweet but they contain good things too, like oats and dried fruit, so I don't feel too bad about the kids eating them. I've suggested my favourite combination, but you can vary the ingredients as you like. These are quite chewy, so if you want them crunchier, bake for another 5 minutes.

Makes 12–16

300g unsalted butter
100g golden syrup
50ml maple syrup
75g light soft brown sugar
350g porridge oats
100g desiccated coconut
200g chocolate chips
100g raisins
100g glacé cherries, halved
salt

1. Preheat your oven to 180°C/160°C fan/gas 4. Line a brownie tin (30 x 20cm) with baking paper.

2. Put the butter, golden syrup, maple syrup and sugar in a large saucepan and melt over a gentle heat. When the sugar has completely dissolved, stir in all the remaining ingredients along with a generous pinch of salt. Mix thoroughly.

3. Pile the mixture into the prepared tin. Spread it as evenly as you can, then – and this bit is important – press it down as firmly as you can. This will help the ingredients stick together better and will give you a less crumbly flapjack.

4. Bake for 25–30 minutes until the flapjacks are golden brown around edges and look slightly puffy.

5. Remove from the oven. Leave to cool for a few minutes, then portion by scoring lines across the top. You should get 12–16 pieces, depending on how big you want them. When the flapjacks are completely cool, cut cleanly along your scored lines. Store them in an airtight tin for up to a week.

SOUPS, SANDWICHES and SALADS

Mmm – sandwiches
are the best

These are all big favourites with my lot. I love a sandwich for lunch or any time really, and I enjoy experimenting with different fillings, while Stacey would eat salad for every meal given the chance. The kids will eat a salad now too – as long as there's something like a bit of cheese in there. Soups are so easy to make and great to have in the fridge, ready for a quick meal.

ONE-POT

FREEZE

Yellowfish Soup

Our kids call smoked haddock 'yellowfish' and they like it in this soup. I'd never had it before until Stacey's mum, Fiona, made it for us. So simple but every spoonful is a mouthful of goodness. You can even add a poached egg to each serving if you like.

Serves 4–6

1 piece of smoked haddock fillet (350–400g)
100ml white wine
2 bay leaves
a few black peppercorns
1 sprig of dill

SOUP

fish or vegetable stock
25g butter
1 large onion, diced
2 celery sticks, diced
2 carrots, diced (peeling optional)
150g piece of squash, peeled and diced
2 leeks, sliced into rounds
200g floury potatoes, such as Maris Pipers or King Edwards, diced (peeling optional)
150g sweetcorn
1 small bunch of dill, finely chopped
salt and black pepper

GARNISH (OPTIONAL)

4–6 poached eggs
1 sprig of dill, finely chopped

1. Put the smoked haddock in a saucepan so it fits in a single layer and pour over the white wine. Add the bay leaves, peppercorns and dill. Cover with cold water and bring to the boil. Remove the pan from the heat and leave to stand for 5 minutes – by this time the fish should be cooked.

2. When the fish is cool enough to handle, transfer it to a board. Measure the poaching liquid and make up it up to 1 litre with fish or vegetable stock. Remove the skin from the fish and pick out any stray bones. Break the flesh into large chunks.

3. Melt the butter in a large saucepan. Add the onion, celery and carrots and season with salt and pepper. Stir until they are all well coated with the butter, then cover and leave to cook over a low heat for about 10 minutes. By this time, the vegetables should be cooked but still have a little bite to them.

4. Add the squash, leeks and potatoes. Stir again, then pour over the poaching liquor and stock mixture. Check the seasoning and add more to taste. Bring to the boil, then turn down the heat and partially cover the pan with a lid. Simmer for 10 minutes. Add the sweetcorn and dill and continue to simmer until the vegetables are all tender.

5. Add the fish to the soup and heat through. Serve piping hot, with a poached egg if you like (see page 26 for how to poach eggs) and more dill.

Leek and Potato Soup

This is one of my favourite soups. It's good at any time of year, but I like to make it after Christmas when we have some cooked ham left over from the feast. It's great made with turkey stock too.

Serves 4-6

30g butter
3 leeks (about 400g), green and
   white parts finely sliced
300g floury potatoes, such as
   Maris Pipers or King Edwards,
   unpeeled and diced
2 garlic cloves, finely chopped
800ml light chicken stock,
   vegetable stock or water
100ml milk
50ml single cream
salt and pepper

TO GARNISH (OPTIONAL)
1 tbsp olive oil
100g cooked ham, shredded
2 tsp maple syrup
chives

1. Melt the butter in a saucepan and add the leeks and potatoes. Season with a generous pinch of salt and stir until the vegetables are well coated with the butter. Cover and leave to cook over a low heat, stirring regularly, until the leeks are completely tender. This will take at least 10 minutes.

2. Add the garlic and cook for another couple of minutes, then pour in the stock or water. Bring to the boil, then turn down the heat, cover the pan and leave to simmer until the potatoes are tender and the flavours have had a chance to blend – another 10 minutes.

3. Using a hand or jug blender, purée the soup. Tip it back into the pan if you've used a jug blender. Add the milk and cream, then reheat gently and check the seasoning. Add a little more salt if necessary and some white or black pepper.

4. To make the ham garnish, heat the olive oil in a frying pan and fry the ham for a few minutes until it starts to crisp. Drizzle over the maple syrup and cook, stirring constantly, until the ham looks crisp and well glazed.

5. Serve the soup sprinkled with the ham, if using, and some finely snipped chives.

ONE-POT

FREEZE

Minestrone

My nan Betty used to cook minestrone for my grandad, and he'd eat it cold as a starter! He swore that was the best way to have it but I prefer mine hot. My grandad was Italian, and he had some strange habits with food – he'd have jam on his cornflakes! I've suggested a nice selection of ingredients here, but this is a great soup for using up odds and ends of veg from the fridge, so feel free to use what you have. You can add frozen vegetables like peas and broad beans and if you've got a piece of Parmesan rind, chuck that in too – it adds extra flavour.

Serves 4-6

1 tbsp olive oil
200g pancetta or bacon lardons (preferably smoked)
1 large onion, chopped
2 large carrots, peeled and diced
3 celery sticks, diced
4 garlic cloves, crushed or grated
400g butternut squash or pumpkin, peeled and cut into chunks
1 tsp dried sage
1 sprig of thyme (or ½ tsp dried thyme)
100ml red or white wine
1.5 litres chicken, vegetable or ham stock
1 tomato, finely diced
a bit of Parmesan rind (optional)
400g tin cannellini or borlotti beans
100g spaghetti or linguine, broken into 3–4cm lengths
200g kale, spring greens or green cabbage, roughly chopped
black pepper

TO SERVE
grated Parmesan
basil pesto (optional)

1. Heat the oil in a large saucepan. Add the pancetta or bacon and fry over a high heat until well browned and some of the fat is coming out.

2. Add the onion, carrots and celery and continue to fry until the vegetables are beginning to brown around the edges. Keep stirring to make sure nothing catches on the bottom of the pan.

3. Stir in the garlic, squash or pumpkin and herbs, then pour in the wine. Bring to the boil and let most of the wine bubble off, then add the stock, tomato and the Parmesan rind if you have one. Bring to the boil, then turn down the heat and partially cover the pan. Leave to simmer for 20 minutes or until the vegetables are tender.

4. Add the beans, pasta and greens and bring to the boil again. Turn the heat down to a simmer and continue to cook until the pasta and greens are tender. Remove the remains of the cheese rind. Serve with plenty of grated Parmesan, spoonfuls of pesto if you like, and black pepper.

Joe's Tip

The pasta will continue to swell as the soup cools, so if you want to make this ahead of time, just prepare it to the end of step 3. When you're nearly ready to eat, add the beans, pasta and greens as in step 4.

ONE-POT

FREEZE

Chicken Stew
with Dumplings

My nanny Fran was Irish, and stews were her thing. My mum learned how to make this from her, and we'd have it on cold winter days. Mum would go to the local butcher, Mori's, and he'd give her nice little cheap cuts for stews. Now I make this with leftover roast chicken as well as fresh, and you can add any odds and ends from Sunday dinner too, such as leftover roast potatoes and parsnips.

Serves 6

1 tbsp olive oil

1 onion, thickly sliced

500g boneless and skinless chicken (preferably thighs), cut into large pieces

4 large carrots, peeled and cut into chunks

3 celery sticks, cut into 3cm lengths

½ swede or celeriac, peeled and diced

3 leeks, cut into 3cm rounds

2 bay leaves

1 sprig of thyme or ½ tsp dried thyme

4 garlic cloves, finely chopped (optional)

1.2 litres chicken stock

100g peas (or any cooked greens)

salt and black pepper

DUMPLINGS

200g self-raising flour

100g suet

1. Heat the olive oil in a large saucepan. Add the onion and chicken, then season with salt and pepper. Fry over a high heat until the chicken is lightly browned.

2. Add the vegetables, herbs and garlic, if using, and stir for a minute or two. Pour over the chicken stock.

3. Bring to the boil, then turn down the heat and cover the pan with a lid. Simmer for about 30 minutes until the vegetables are completely tender. Check for seasoning and add the peas or any other greens.

4. To make the dumplings, put the flour and suet in a bowl with a generous pinch of salt. Add just enough water to mix to a firm, slightly sticky dough.

5. Pull the dough into 6 pieces (it will be sticky but having wet hands will help) and drop them on top of the stew. Cover the pan again and leave to simmer for another 15 minutes. The dumplings with puff up and take on a glossy sheen.

ONE-POT

FREEZE

Tomato *and* Vegetable Soup

If I was off school ill when I was a child, my mum would give me tinned tomato soup for lunch, so I thought it was something you only had when you were poorly. I connect it with sitting indoors, not feeling great but still nice and warm and secure, having my soup. I make my own now and it has a similar lovely flavour but with all the extra veg, it's better for you than tinned. I like to serve it with a lump of cheese in the middle of the hot soup. The cheese melts and goes all gooey and delicious.

Serves 4-6

2 tbsp olive oil
1 large onion, chopped
2 large carrots, chopped
   (peeling optional)
2 celery sticks, chopped
200g squash or pumpkin, peeled
   and chopped
4 garlic cloves, chopped
2 sprigs of basil, left whole
1 tsp dried herbs
800ml vegetable stock or water
2 x 400g tins chopped tomatoes
30g butter
pinch of sugar (optional)
salt and black pepper

TO SERVE
4–6 thick slices of Cheddar
   cheese or similar

1. Heat the olive oil in a large saucepan. Add the vegetables and cook over a high heat for several minutes until starting to brown around the edges.

2. Add the garlic, basil and dried herbs, and season with salt and pepper. Pour over the stock or water and bring to the boil. Simmer for 5 minutes, covered, just so the vegetables start softening before the tomatoes are added.

3. Add the tomatoes and bring back to the boil. Turn the heat down again, cover the pan with a lid and leave to simmer for 30 minutes or until the vegetables are completely tender.

4. Add the butter to the soup. When it has melted, purée the soup in a blender until smooth, then reheat until piping hot.

5. To serve, put a chunk of cheese in each bowl and pour the soup over it. Leave to stand for a couple of minutes to allow the cheese to start melting, then enjoy.

Joe's Tip

The squash and basil bring sweetness to this soup, so even if the tomatoes are a bit acidic, you shouldn't need to add any sugar. Give it a taste and you can add a pinch at the end if necessary once it's blended.

My nan

My mum's mum, known to us all as Little Nanny Frannie, came to live with us for nearly two years after my dad died when I was 11.

Mum was on her own with us and she had to become the breadwinner too. Nan looked after us, including Mum, and made sure we were fed and went to school. She was so special, and we were so lucky to have her. She was exactly what we needed at that time.

For me, she was my rock, my constant, my go-to person. She gave me the attention and love I needed – and more than anything the time I needed. I wouldn't cry in front of my mum and my sisters. Everyone wanted me to have counselling because I wouldn't cry, but my nan was the only person I felt I could break down with. I didn't want to show any weakness to my mum and sisters and in fact, I resented it sometimes when they were crying and showing their grief. I couldn't deal with them being in so much pain. But with Nan it was different. I'd talk things through with her and I always felt better after we'd spent time together.

I don't know what we would have done without Nan during that time. But as soon as she felt we could all manage and my mum was getting a bit better and moving on, she went back home. We didn't want her to go, but she knew it was time and that we would survive on our own. She had that wisdom.

Nan was only five foot two inches tall, but she could be fierce and feisty. My mum was her eldest daughter – she had six kids – and I was the eldest of her grandchildren, so we had a very special bond. Although to be honest, we all thought we were special to her. One time my cousin Charlie phoned her up and said, 'Hello, Nan'. She said, 'Who's that?' and he replied, 'It's your favourite grandson'. And Nan immediately said, 'Oh, hello Joe'.

I was always known as her favourite. I adored her and, apart from my mum, she was the most important person in my life. When I was grown up, I'd still phone her and pour my heart out to her when I had troubles. She always made me feel secure, loved and safe. And she was so proud of me when I was on *EastEnders*. She lived in Thetford in Norfolk, and she'd go round with her bag stuffed with autographed pictures of me to give anyone who asked. When I went to see her, I always had to go and meet all her friends. She loved that her grandson was on the telly.

Nan passed away in 2021 and I miss her more than I can say. I've got this way of putting things in little drawers and trying not to think about them – like when my dad died. But every now and then memories of my nan pop into my head and I feel like she's still here with me. It breaks my heart.

It was during Covid, and she died on her own in hospital. None of us were allowed to see her in her last days. She had 32 grandkids and 15 great-grandkids, but only a few of us could go to her funeral. It should have been huge – she had such a big family and like a lot of older people she used to talk about what an occasion her funeral would be. I can't imagine anyone has ever had a better, more loving grandparent than my Little Nan.

Memories of my nan pop in to my head and I feel like she's still here with me

Sloppy Joe Sandwiches

I used to love Friday nights when my dad would come back from work, knowing he'd be home for a couple of days. I was like his shadow and would follow him around all the time. Once he was home, we'd get fish and chips or another takeaway and watch *Roseanne* – that American TV sitcom. At some point in the series, Roseanne had a café that served Sloppy Joes, but I didn't really know what they were. Then one time my mum made them for us to eat while we watched the show. Great memories.

Serves 4

1 tbsp olive oil
1 large onion, finely chopped
1 red pepper, finely diced
1 green pepper, finely diced
400g beef mince
4 garlic cloves, finely chopped
1 tsp onion powder
1 tsp dried oregano or mixed herbs
2 tbsp tomato purée
2 tsp Dijon mustard
1–2 tsp hot sauce, plus extra to serve
1 tsp Worcestershire sauce
2 tsp cider vinegar
1 tbsp dark or light soy sauce
200g chopped tomatoes (tinned are best)
200ml beef stock or water
1 tbsp BBQ sauce (optional, to taste)
salt and black pepper

TO SERVE
4 burger buns, or lengths of baguette
75g Cheddar cheese, grated
lettuce leaves

1. Heat the oil in a large saucepan and add the onion and peppers. Cook gently over a low–medium heat, stirring regularly, until the onion starts to look translucent.

2. Turn up the heat and add the beef mince. Break it up with the tip of a wooden spoon and stir until it has browned. Add the garlic, onion powder, dried herbs and tomato purée and cook for another couple of minutes, stirring constantly.

3. Add the mustard, hot sauce, Worcestershire sauce, cider vinegar, soy sauce, tomatoes and stock or water. Season with salt and pepper and bring to the boil. Turn the heat down to a low simmer and cover the pan. Cook for 20 minutes, stirring every so often.

4. Remove the lid and continue to cook until the mixture has reduced, stirring regularly to prevent the base from sticking. You want the texture to be nice and thick so it will hold together reasonably well in a sandwich.

5. Taste and add the BBQ sauce if you would like a smokier flavour, and more hot sauce if you want extra heat. Simmer for another few minutes.

6. Heat the grill to medium–high. Toast the buns or baguette, then squash the inside of one piece so it makes a hollow to pile the meat into. Add the sloppy Joe mix and sprinkle with cheese. Heat under the grill until the cheese has melted, then add lettuce and top with the remaining slices of bread.

Joe's Tip *A bit of crunch is good in this, so you could add some crisps on top of the meat mix, or some sliced pickled onions.*

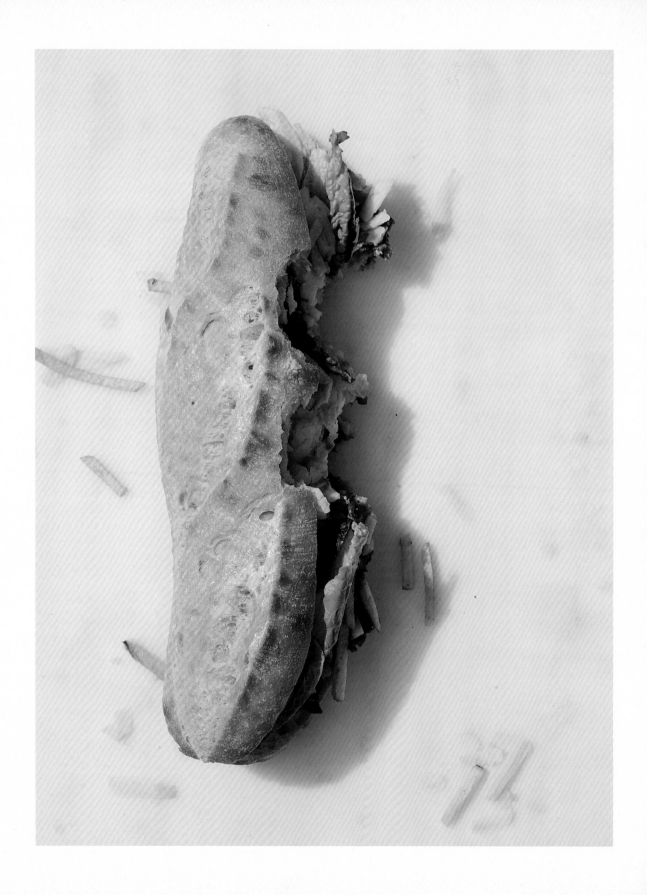

QUICK

ONE-POT

Club Sandwich

I've been told that you can always judge hotel room service by the quality of its club sandwich. I presented the *I'm a Celebrity...* spin-off show for 10 years and I'm not joking – I used to eat a club sandwich every day. I loved them so much. At the end of the two months, my hotel bill would be 80 per cent club sandwiches. One year, the chef changed, and I was so devastated the hotel manager said I could come down to the kitchen and show them how to prepare the sandwich how I wanted it. The key to success when you're making them yourself is to get the chicken, avocado and salad all ready before frying the eggs and toasting the bread.

Makes 2 Sandwiches*

*to serve 2 hungry people, or 4 less hungry with extra salad and crisps

1 large cooked chicken breast
½ large or 1 small avocado
squeeze of lemon juice
6 slices of bread
butter, for spreading and frying
1 handful of lettuce or salad
   leaves, roughly torn
2 eggs
a wedge of Brie
salt and black pepper

TO SERVE
crisps
salad (optional)

1. Thinly slice the chicken breast – the best thing to do is to cut it slightly on the diagonal. Season with a little salt and pepper.

2. Thinly slice the avocado. Squeeze lemon juice over the chicken and the avocado.

3. Toast 4 of the slices of bread. Butter the toast if you like, and divide the lettuce, chicken and avocado between 2 of the slices. Top with other 2 slices of toast.

4. Fry the eggs while you toast the remaining 2 slices of bread. Add an egg to each sandwich and season again with more salt and pepper.

5. If the Brie is very ripe, spread it over the final slices of toast before completing the sandwiches. If the Brie is firmer, cut it into thin slices and arrange over the egg, then top with the final slices of toast.

6. Cut the sandwiches into halves or quarters and secure with cocktail sticks. Serve immediately with crisps and salad, if you like.

ONE-POT

FREEZE

Chicken Nugget Wraps

It's worth making plenty of these chicken nuggets, as they keep well for a couple of days and make great little lunchbox treats or quick snacks. Marinating the chicken in buttermilk makes it beautifully tender and I like to make a buttermilk dressing to add to the wraps.

Makes 4

4 skinless chicken breast fillets
250ml buttermilk
2 garlic cloves, crushed
1 tsp dried oregano
25g butter, melted, or 2 tbsp
   olive oil
salt

COATING

50g plain flour
1 tsp garlic or onion powder
½ tsp smoked paprika
2 eggs
100g panko breadcrumbs

BUTTERMILK DRESSING

35–50ml buttermilk (depending
   on pot size)
2 tbsp mayonnaise
squeeze of lemon juice
½ tsp garlic powder
½ tsp dried oregano or
   mixed herbs
a few chives, finely snipped

TO SERVE

½ romaine lettuce or 1 large Little
   Gem, shredded
¼ cucumber, thinly sliced
4 wraps
2 tomatoes, diced

1. First slice the chicken into thick strips, cutting widthways but at a slight angle to make them longer. Sprinkle with salt.

2. Mix the 250ml of buttermilk, garlic and oregano together in a bowl. Add the chicken and cover. Leave to marinate in the fridge for at least 1 hour – or overnight if that works better for you, timing-wise.

3. When you are ready to cook the chicken, preheat the oven to 200°C/180°C fan/gas 6. Put the flour in a shallow bowl with the garlic or onion powder and the smoked paprika. Season with salt.

4. Break one of the eggs into another shallow bowl and beat thoroughly. Put half the panko breadcrumbs in another bowl.

5. Remove the chicken from its marinade and scrape off any excess. Dip the strips in the flour mixture, toss to coat and then pat off any excess. Repeat with the egg and finally the breadcrumbs, making sure they are well coated. When you have used up all of first batch of egg and breadcrumbs, add the rest to the bowls – this way, things don't get too messy.

6. Place the coated chicken strips on a baking tray lined with baking paper. Brush with a little melted butter or oil. Bake in the oven for about 15 minutes or until the coating is crisp and golden.

7. Mix all the dressing ingredients together and season with salt and pepper.

8. To assemble, arrange some lettuce and cucumber in a line in the centre of a wrap. Top with some tomato, then arrange the chicken over the top. Drizzle with some of the dressing.

9. Fold in the two shorter sides of each wrap. Fold over one of the longer sides, then roll until the filling is completely enclosed. Serve at once.

Joe's Tip

If you make these for lunchboxes, it's best to let the chicken cool down a little first before wrapping. My kids also like to have the dressing in a little pot, so the wrap doesn't go soggy.

Coronation Chicken Sandwich

This is Stacey's favourite sandwich and I make it for her often. When she was pregnant, she just loved these flavours, and I would make her a salad of raw cauliflower with coronation sauce. She ate bowlfuls of it and it became her go-to pregnancy dish.

Makes 4 Sandwiches

FILLING
50g mayonnaise
50g Greek yoghurt
2 tsp mild curry powder
2 tbsp mango chutney
1 tsp hot sauce (or to taste)
squeeze of lemon juice
1 celery stick, finely chopped
2 spring onions, finely chopped
2 large cooked chicken
   breasts, diced
salt and black pepper

PICKLED CUCUMBER
½ cucumber, thinly sliced
1 tbsp white wine vinegar
½ tsp caster sugar
½ tsp salt

TO FINISH
butter
8 slices of bread or
   4 bagels, halved
lettuce or salad leaves

1. First make the pickled cucumber. Put the cucumber in a colander. Mix the vinegar with the sugar and ½ teaspoon of salt, then pour this over the cucumber and toss to combine. Leave to stand for 30 minutes, then blot the cucumber slices with a tea towel or on kitchen paper.

2. Put all the ingredients for the filling in a bowl and season with salt and pepper. Mix thoroughly.

3. Butter the bread or bagel halves and make up the sandwiches with the filling, pickled cucumber and some lettuce or other salad leaves.

ONE-POT

Chicken Caesar Salad

For me, salads are all to do with Stacey. She'll eat anything in her salads as long as there's some crunch, so this one is just right. She'll even eat salad without any dressing – she could easily be a rabbit. I enjoy making this and I like pounding the anchovies to make the dressing. You can, of course, use ready-cooked chicken, but this way of preparing it works brilliantly and the meat is lovely and tender.

Serves 4

CHICKEN

2 large skinless chicken breast
   fillets (or 4 thigh fillets)
2 tbsp olive oil
zest of 1 lemon, plus juice
   of ½ lemon
1 garlic clove, crushed
1 tsp dried thyme or oregano,
   or mixed herbs
salt and black pepper

SALAD

4 anchovy fillets, finely chopped
1 garlic clove, crushed
juice of ½ lemon
2 tsp red wine vinegar
4 tbsp olive oil
1 heaped tsp tarragon or
   Dijon mustard
2 romaine lettuces, roughly torn
25g Parmesan or similar, grated
croutons (see page 272)

1. First prepare the chicken. If using chicken breasts, put each breast on a board and holding it flat with one hand, slice through it horizontally from the side. You will end up with 4 thinner pieces with the same surface area.

2. Put the olive oil, lemon zest and juice, garlic and herbs into a bowl with ½ teaspoon of salt and a crack of black pepper. Whisk everything together, then add the chicken, making sure it is well coated. Cover and leave to marinate in the fridge for at least 1 hour – or overnight if you like.

3. When you are ready to cook the chicken, heat a griddle until medium–hot and add the chicken. Cook for a few minutes on each side until cooked through (you can test with a thermometer if you like, it should read 74°C in the thickest part of the meat) and has deep char lines. Remove and leave to cool to room temperature, then slice into strips.

4. To make the salad, put the anchovies and garlic in the base of a salad bowl and mash them together. Add the lemon juice, vinegar, oil and tarragon or Dijon mustard and whisk thoroughly until they are blended together.

5. Add the lettuce and sprinkle in the cheese. Mix thoroughly with salad serving spoons – the cheese will mix with the dressing to give the lettuce a creamy coating. Divide between 4 bowls and top with the chicken and croutons.

QUICK

ONE-POT

Ham *and* Cheese Chopped Salad

The kids like this. They won't eat a plain leafy salad but put some ham and cheese in with the greens and they're happy. You have to chop the ham and cheese up really small so they can't pick it out and they have to eat the lot! That's the trick.

Serves 4

200g tomatoes, diced
½ large cucumber, diced
2 celery sticks, diced
100g radishes, sliced
1 large carrot, coarsely grated
  (peeling optional)
6 spring onions, finely sliced
1 raw beetroot, peeled and
  coarsely grated (optional)
100g sweetcorn (optional)
50g mixed salad leaves, shredded
1 large romaine or cos lettuce,
  shredded
200g cauliflower or broccoli
  florets
50g gherkins, finely chopped
150g ham, diced or shredded
100g cheese, finely diced or grated
1 large sprig of tarragon, leaves
  picked and finely chopped
½ tsp mixed dried herbs

DRESSING
100g mayonnaise
30g ketchup
1 tsp onion or garlic powder
2 tsp gherkin pickle liquid
dash of Worcestershire sauce
dash of hot sauce such as Tabasco
squeeze of lemon juice (optional)
salt and black pepper

TO GARNISH
smoked paprika or cayenne
  pepper

1. Put the tomatoes, cucumber, celery, radishes, carrot, spring onions, beetroot and sweetcorn, if using, into a large salad bowl. Add the mixed salad leaves and the lettuce.

2. Bring a saucepan of water to the boil and add the cauliflower or broccoli. Cook for just 2 minutes, then drain and refresh under cold water. Roughly chop. Add to the salad bowl along with the gherkins, ham, cheese and herbs.

3. Mix the salad dressing by whisking the mayonnaise, ketchup and onion or garlic powder together, then add the pickle liquid, Worcestershire sauce and hot sauce. Add salt and pepper and taste, then squeeze in some lemon juice if you think the dressing needs it.

4. Toss all the salad ingredients together and divide between 4 bowls. Drizzle over the dressing or serve in a jug for people to add for themselves. Sprinkle the smoked paprika or cayenne over the salad and serve immediately.

Steak Salad

Stacey loves salads, I love steak, so this recipe is perfect as it combines our two favourites. And it's great way of making two steaks serve four people.

Serves 4

1 red onion, thinly sliced into crescents
juice of 1 lime
400g small new potatoes, unpeeled and halved
2 tbsp olive oil
2 sprigs of rosemary, finely chopped
4 garlic cloves, unpeeled
200g green beans, trimmed
2 sirloin steaks or similar
1 tsp mixed dried herbs
200g mixed salad leaves
300g cherry tomatoes, halved
a few fresh herbs (tarragon or basil and chives), finely chopped or snipped
salt and black pepper

DRESSING

3 tbsp olive oil
1 tbsp sherry vinegar
1 tsp wholegrain mustard
1 tsp honey

1. First, sprinkle the red onion with salt and cover with the lime juice. Leave to stand for 30 minutes – this helps reduce any bitterness.

2. Cook the potatoes. Preheat the oven to 200°C/180°C fan/gas 6. Put the potatoes in a saucepan, cover them with water and add salt. Bring to the boil, simmer for about 10–12 minutes until tender, then drain.

3. Tip the potatoes into a roasting tin and drizzle over the olive oil. Sprinkle over the rosemary and add the garlic cloves. Roast for about 20 minutes until crisp and browned.

4. Bring a saucepan of water to the boil and add salt. Add the green beans and cook for several minutes until just tender. Drain and refresh in cold water.

5. Heat a griddle pan until it is too hot to hold your hand over. Sprinkle the steaks with salt, pepper and the mixed herbs. Cook for several minutes on each side, turning regularly, until lightly charred and just pink. Transfer to a chopping board and leave to stand for 5 minutes, then thinly slice.

6. To make the dressing, whisk together the olive oil, sherry vinegar, mustard and honey. Drain the red onions and add the lime juice to the dressing. Check for seasoning and add as necessary.

7. To assemble, arrange the potatoes, beans, salad leaves and tomatoes over a large platter or 4 individual salad bowls. Drizzle over most of the dressing and toss gently. Top with the sliced steak, onion slices and more dressing, and garnish with any fresh herbs.

Halloumi Salad

My mum was a fan of halloumi before it was as popular as it is now – we called it squeaky cheese and my children do too. This recipe is a bit like a Greek salad, but with my special extras, like bacon bits. If you like this, try making double of the bacon bits, pitta croutons and dressing to keep in the fridge for another time.

Serves 4

1 small red onion, finely sliced
4 tbsp olive oil
1 garlic clove, crushed
2 pitta breads, roughly cut up
100g smoked streaky bacon
2 x 225–250g blocks of halloumi, cut into slices
1 tsp dried mint
a few chilli flakes (optional)
½ large cucumber, cut into chunks
250g tomatoes, halved or quartered depending on size
1 red pepper, diced
¼ red cabbage, shredded
2 large Little Gem lettuces or 1 heart of romaine, roughly chopped

DRESSING

4 tbsp olive oil
juice of ½ lemon
1 tsp sherry vinegar
1 tsp dried oregano
½ tsp honey
salt and black pepper

1. Sprinkle the red onion with salt and cover with cold water. Leave to stand for 30 minutes. This helps to reduce any bitterness.

2. Make the pitta croutons. Preheat the oven to 200°C/180°C fan/gas 6. Put 2 tablespoons of the olive oil in a bowl and add the garlic. Add the pieces of pitta and toss thoroughly. Arrange them on a baking tray and bake in the oven for about 10 minutes until crisped up.

3. Heat a tablespoon of the oil in a frying pan and fry the bacon over a medium heat until crisp and brown on both sides. You will find plenty of fat will render out. Drain the slices on kitchen paper, then chop very finely.

4. Whisk all the ingredients for the dressing together with a pinch of salt and freshly ground black pepper.

5. Now grill the halloumi. Heat a griddle pan until it's too hot to hold your hand over. Toss the halloumi with the remaining olive oil, the dried mint and the chilli flakes, if using. Grill the halloumi on both sides until soft and marked with dark char lines.

6. Put the cucumber, tomatoes, red pepper, red cabbage and lettuce in a large salad bowl and add the drained red onion and the pitta croutons. Add the dressing and toss thoroughly. Divide between 4 large salad bowls or plates. Top with the slices of halloumi and garnish with the bacon bits.

Joe's Tip

Halloumi is really good in a pitta sandwich. Grill as above. Lightly toast the pittas and cut them in half, to open like a pocket. Pile in the halloumi with cucumber, lettuce and tomato. Mix 150g yoghurt with 1 teaspoon of dried mint and a pinch of ground cinnamon and drizzle this over as a dressing.

WEEKDAYS

A family meal is my happy place

After a busy day, I love that we all sit down for a family meal together in the evening. My kids are pretty good eaters on the whole, but sometimes it can be a struggle to come up with dishes that everyone loves. This chapter includes some of my sure-fire winners, like turkey burgers, katsu chicken and traybakes – meals that the kids enjoy which are also healthy and nutritious.

Curried Cauliflower Cheese

This is my special take on cauli cheese – I add a spoonful of curry powder which really peps it up and makes it extra tasty. I like to put in any of the cauliflower leaves that are in a good state as well as the florets – no reason to waste them. All the family enjoy this dish with a Sunday roast or on its own and Stacey likes a dollop of mango chutney on the side!

Serves 4–6

1 large cauliflower
50g butter
1 small onion or shallot, very
  finely diced
1 garlic clove, crushed
1 tsp mustard seeds
1 tbsp mild curry powder
50g plain flour
600ml milk
75g mature Cheddar, grated
salt and black pepper

TO FINISH
50g mature Cheddar, grated

1. Take the leaves off the cauliflower, chuck out any that don't look too good, then thickly slice the rest. Break the cauliflower up into florets.

2. Put the cauliflower in a steamer basket. Place the steamer over a pan of simmering water and steam until the florets are tender when pierced with a sharp knife. This will take 6–8 minutes. Remove the steamer from the pan and set aside.

3. Preheat your oven to 180°C/160°C fan/gas 4.

4. For the sauce, melt the butter in a saucepan and add the diced onion or shallot. Fry over a medium–high heat for a few minutes until starting to soften, then add the garlic and mustard seeds. Season with salt and pepper, then cook for another minute.

5. Add the curry powder and flour, then cook, stirring constantly, until you have a thick paste. Add about a quarter of the milk and stir thoroughly – the mixture will thicken up and will come away from the base of the saucepan.

6. Gradually add the rest of the milk, stirring constantly between each addition, until you have a sauce that has the consistency of thick double cream. Add the cheese and stir until it has melted.

7. Put the cauliflower into an ovenproof dish and pour over the sauce. Top with the grated cheese. Bake in the oven for about 25 minutes until bubbling and well browned on top.

ONE-POT

Salmon, Pesto *and* Spinach Tart

The kids love a bit of salmon. You can make this recipe even quicker if you buy the pesto, but it is good to make your own. It's nicer for one thing and this version works well with the tart, as I use a little less oil than usual because of the oily salmon and rich pastry. The lemon zest adds a touch of freshness. The pesto keeps for a week in the fridge.

Serves 4–6

250g fresh spinach
1 x 320g pack of ready-rolled
   puff pastry
1 egg, beaten with a little water
300g salmon fillet, skinned and
   cut into large irregular chunks
8 cherry tomatoes, halved
zest of 1 lemon
a few basil leaves
1 tbsp olive oil
up to 1 tbsp balsamic vinegar
squeeze of lemon juice
sea salt and black pepper

PESTO
2 tbsp pine nuts or almonds
½ garlic clove, crushed
1 large bunch of basil,
   leaves picked
10g Parmesan, finely grated
zest of 1 lemon and a squeeze
   of juice
50ml olive oil

1. Start with the pesto. Put the pine nuts in a food processor and pulse until quite finely chopped. Add the garlic, basil leaves, Parmesan, lemon zest and a large pinch of sea salt and continue to pulse until the basil is well broken down. Drizzle in the oil with the food processor going until you have a bright, green-flecked sauce. Stir in a squeeze of lemon juice and season to taste. Set aside.

2. Wash the spinach thoroughly and put it in a saucepan while it's still wet. Place the pan over a medium heat and cook the spinach, pressing it down with a wooden spoon, until it has wilted down. Drain in a colander. When the spinach is cool enough to handle, squeeze it gently to remove the excess liquid.

3. Preheat your oven to 200°C/180°C fan/gas 6. Unroll the pastry and place it on a large baking tray lined with baking paper. Score a 2cm border around the pastry, making sure you cut deeply, but not quite all the way through. Prick the centre of the pastry all over with a fork, then brush it with the beaten egg.

4. Put the pastry in the oven and bake for 15 minutes. When you take the pastry out, you'll see that the centre will have puffed up a little as well as the sides. It will go down a bit as the pastry cools – press it down gently with a spoon or the flat of your hand to help it on its way. Leave the oven on.

5. To assemble, spread 3 tablespoons of the pesto over the tart. Top with the spinach, then arrange the pieces of salmon and the cherry tomatoes on top. Grate over lemon zest and tuck in a few basil leaves.

6. Whisk the oil and vinegar together and brush the mixture over the salmon and the cut sides of the cherry tomatoes.

7. Bake the tart for another 10 minutes or until the salmon and tomatoes are cooked through and the pastry is a rich golden brown. You can brush a little extra pesto over the top, if you like.

Fish Fingers *with* Pea Purée *and* Tartar Sauce

I always ate fish fingers when I was growing up – in a sandwich, with some chips – and my kids love them too. But then I decided to start making my own instead of buying them – they're healthier and a different taste sensation. The kids have them with a bit of tartar sauce and these mashed-up peas and it's a winner.

Serves 4

FISH FINGERS
500g cod or haddock loin, trimmed
50g plain flour
1–2 eggs
100g panko breadcrumbs
2 tbsp olive oil or 25g melted butter, for brushing
salt and black pepper

PEA PURÉE
15g butter
1 small onion, finely chopped
1 tsp dried mint
400g frozen peas, defrosted

TARTAR SAUCE
100g mayonnaise or 50g mayonnaise plus 50g thick yoghurt
6 small gherkins or cornichons (about 50g), finely chopped
2 tbsp capers, chopped
zest and juice of ½ lime
leaves from 3 sprigs of tarragon, finely chopped
1 tsp Dijon or tarragon mustard (optional)

TO SERVE (OPTIONAL)
white farmhouse bread or baps, for sandwiches

1. To make the fish fingers, lay out the fish loin and trim it if it isn't completely rectangular. Cut it into 4 long strips (lengthways), then cut each strip into 3 pieces.

2. Put the flour, one egg and half the breadcrumbs into separate bowls. Season the flour with salt and pepper and beat the egg. It's good to use just one of the eggs to start with as, depending on size, that may be enough to coat all the fish.

3. Dip the fish into the flour, dust off, then dip into the egg followed by the breadcrumbs. Replenish the egg and breadcrumbs as necessary.

4. Place the fish fingers onto a lined baking tray and chill them until ready to cook. You could also freeze them at this point.

5. When you are ready to cook, preheat your oven to 200°C/180°C fan/ gas 6. Brush the fish fingers with oil or melted butter and bake them in the oven for about 15 minutes until cooked through with a crisp, lightly golden coating.

6. To make the pea purée, melt the butter in a small pan and add the onion. Cook gently until soft and translucent, then add the mint and peas along with plenty of seasoning. Add a splash of water – no more than about 50ml – and cover the pan. Simmer for a few minutes until the peas are cooked but still bright green and bouncy. Purée and set aside.

7. To make the tartar sauce, mix all the ingredients together, including the mustard, if using, and season with salt and pepper.

8. Serve the fish fingers with the pea purée and tartar sauce or make them into sandwiches.

EastEnders

I'd started going to Anna Scher's drama school while my dad was still alive. It was just round the corner from us and geared towards working-class kids in the community. Linda Robson was a friend of my mum's and she'd been to the school and thought I'd like it and do well. I went to classes after normal school on Fridays and on Saturdays, and I guess it was a good way of keeping me entertained and out of trouble.

When my dad died, I had to give up my football. I used to train a few times a week and my dad would always come with me, but none of my uncles would take me so I had to knock that on the head. By that time, I was at secondary school, and I realized I wasn't going to be academic, so instead, I threw myself more into my acting. When I was about 15, I got a part in a play at the National Theatre – *The Day I Stood Still*. We had no money at the time, so I was doing a paper round in the morning, then going to school and leaving after lunch to go and do the play – juggling three jobs really.

One day, Julia Crampsie, a casting director on *EastEnders*, came to the theatre to see the play and afterwards she sat down with me and my mum and said I was on her radar for the programme. But I didn't hear anything for years. Then finally I got a call to go and audition for a part as Alfie Moon's brother, Spencer. I was down to the last two but didn't get the part. Then they called me back a year later. It was for a small part – just three episodes – and I wasn't too sure about doing it – I was holding out for a regular part – but I took it. I did another three episodes, then some more and this went on for a year and a half.

I was about 20 years old by then and it was only part-time work, so I was also doing fire protection to earn some more money. I was part of a crew working at the BBC White City and we'd go into the offices to make them fire safe. It was a weird time, juggling two worlds. At the beginning of the week, I'd be on the show, then I'd go into work and the other builders would say, 'You're that boy off *EastEnders*! What are you doing here?' I remember sitting down with my mum and my nan and saying that I wanted to do the Knowledge like my dad, and I wanted to join the fire service, but I'd give *EastEnders* another couple of months.

Then the BBC offered me a contract. They brought in a family around my character, and I was in the show for five years. It was such a great time. My younger sister Shana auditioned under another name for a part as my screen sister and got it. So she was there on set with my mum chaperoning her and I loved it. I loved us all working together. Finally, life was going well again for the family.

JOE SWASH
as Mickey Miller

EastEnders

EastEnders

SHANA SWASH
as Demi Miller

But then things changed completely. I got ill with meningoencephalitis and had to take more than a year off work. I was in intensive care for four weeks, remained in hospital for six months and had to learn to talk and walk properly again. It hit me really badly. When I got back to *EastEnders* the producers had changed and I wasn't getting any storylines. Finally they told me I would be written out of the show in three months.

I was devastated. But when one door shuts another opens. Three months later I was in Australia doing *I'm a Celebrity*… and life changed for ever.

Finally, life was going well again for my family

Mushroom Risotto

I didn't like mushrooms as a child and wouldn't eat them. Much later, when I was in the Jungle for *I'm a Celebrity...*, the basket would come down with everyone's food and it would be kangaroo tail or something. But Timmy Mallett, another contestant, was a vegetarian and he'd be given some wild mushrooms. He'd fry them up and I just had to try some – they smelled so good. I loved them and after that poor old Timmy had to share his mushrooms with me every night. Now, one of my favourite things is a good mushroom risotto.

Serves 4-6

1 tbsp olive oil
50g butter
1 small onion or shallot, finely
   chopped
1 leek, finely chopped
300g mushrooms (white/button/
   cremini/chestnut), finely
   chopped
4 garlic cloves, very finely
   chopped
1 large sprig of thyme,
   leaves picked
400g risotto rice
100ml white wine or Vermouth
1.5 litres chicken or mushroom
   stock
50g Parmesan, grated, plus
   extra to serve
salt and black pepper

TO GARNISH
15g butter
250g mixed mushrooms,
   sliced if large
2 garlic cloves, crushed or
   finely chopped

1. Heat the olive oil and half the butter in a large sauté pan. Add the onion or shallot and the leek and cook very gently, stirring regularly, until soft and translucent.

2. Add the mushrooms to the pan. Turn up the heat and fry until they have given out their liquid and look dry but glossy. Add the garlic and thyme and stir for a couple more minutes.

3. Add the rice and stir for a couple of minutes until glossy with butter. Season with salt and pepper. Pour in the wine or Vermouth and let it bubble away until almost completely evaporated.

4. Add a large ladleful of the hot stock. Stir constantly but slowly until most of the liquid has been absorbed by the rice, then continue to add ladlefuls of stock in the same way until the rice has plumped up and is al dente and the sauce around it is creamy. You may have a small amount of the stock left.

5. Add the remaining butter and the Parmesan and beat it into the risotto – this will make the risotto extra creamy. Taste and adjust the seasoning if necessary. Cover and keep warm.

6. Place a frying pan over a high heat and add the butter. When it is foaming, add the mixed mushrooms and fry them very quickly until well browned. Add the garlic and stir for a couple of minutes, then season with salt and pepper.

7. Serve the risotto garnished with the mushrooms and more grated Parmesan for people to add at the table.

Katsu Chicken

When I first started going out with Stacey, she loved to eat at Wagamama. I didn't think it was my sort of thing until I tried the katsu chicken, which I loved. Now I cook it at home and it's popular with the kids. I normally serve it with plain rice and maybe some broccoli, dressed up with a bit of soy sauce – the boys will eat it that way.

Serves 4

2 large skinless chicken breasts
50g plain flour
1 tsp garlic or onion powder
¼ tsp cayenne pepper or paprika
2 eggs
50g panko breadcrumbs
2 tbsp olive oil
15g butter
salt and black pepper

SAUCE
15g butter or coconut oil
1 onion, finely chopped
1 carrot, grated (peeling optional)
3 garlic cloves, crushed
10g fresh ginger, peeled and grated
1 tbsp medium curry powder
1 tbsp mango chutney
1 tbsp dark or light soy sauce
1 tsp sugar
400ml chicken stock

TO SERVE
rice
a few sprigs of coriander (optional)
lemon wedges

1. First prepare the chicken, cutting each breast in half to make 4 flat pieces. To do this, put one of the breasts on a chopping board. Hold it in place with one hand and cut through from the side, horizontally. Next, put each piece of chicken between 2 pieces of clingfilm and use a meat tenderizing mallet or a rolling pin to bash it until it is very thin. Repeat with the other chicken breast.

2. Put the flour in a shallow bowl with the garlic or onion powder, cayenne or paprika and plenty of salt and pepper. Break the eggs into another bowl and beat until smooth. Put the panko breadcrumbs in a third bowl.

3. Dip each piece of chicken into the flour, then dust off any excess. Next, dip into the egg, making sure it is completely coated, then into the breadcrumbs, flipping over and pressing down to make sure the breadcrumbs stick well.

4. Line a baking tray with baking paper and arrange the chicken pieces over it. Leave in the fridge until you are ready to cook.

5. To make the sauce, heat the butter or coconut oil in a saucepan and add the onion and carrot. Cook over a medium–low heat until the onion is soft and translucent. Add the garlic and ginger, then continue to cook for another 2–3 minutes.

6. Stir in the curry powder, followed by the mango chutney, soy sauce and sugar, then pour in the stock. Slowly bring to the boil, stirring constantly, then simmer for a few minutes until the onions are completely tender. Transfer to a blender or use a stick blender and purée the sauce until smooth. Reheat before serving.

7. To cook the chicken, heat the oil and butter in a frying pan. When the butter foams, add the chicken pieces and cook for 3–4 minutes on each side until cooked through and the breadcrumb coating is crisp and golden brown. Drain on kitchen paper and serve with the sauce over rice, garnished with the coriander if using, and a lemon wedge alongside.

FREEZE

Turkey Burgers

If you put the word burger in front of anything, the kids will have it and turkey mince makes a nice healthy alternative to beef. It's cheap as well. I like to add this BBQ sauce as it makes the burgers good and juicy with a touch of caramelization on the outside.

Makes 4 Big Burgers*

* or 8–12 sliders

400g turkey mince
½ onion, very finely chopped
2 tsp garlic powder
1 tsp dried oregano
75g fresh breadcrumbs
1 egg
dash of Worcestershire sauce
salt and black pepper

BBQ SAUCE
15g butter
½ small onion, finely chopped
1 tsp garlic powder
100g tomato ketchup
15g dark brown sugar
1 tbsp maple syrup
1 tbsp dark or light soy sauce
1 tsp chipotle paste or
   1 tsp smoked paprika
1 tsp Worcestershire sauce
2 tsp red wine vinegar

TO ASSEMBLE
olive or vegetable oil, for frying
slices of cheese
burger buns
lettuce leaves
sliced tomato
sliced red onion
ketchup or other condiments

1. First make the burgers. Mix all the ingredients together and season with plenty of salt and pepper. Knead the mixture with your hands until it starts to feel firmer, then divide and shape into 4 burgers or 8–12 sliders. Chill for at least 30 minutes to firm up a bit.

2. Next, make the BBQ sauce. Melt the butter in a small pan and add the onion. Cook over a gentle heat until soft and translucent, stirring regularly. Transfer to a mini food processor with a splash of water and blend until smooth. Tip it back into the saucepan and add all the remaining ingredients. Heat gently until the sugar has dissolved, stirring constantly, then bring to the boil for a few moments. Remove from the heat.

3. To fry the burgers, heat a little oil in a large frying pan. Add as many of the burgers as you have room for. Cook for 3–4 minutes until a crust has developed on the underside.

4. Flip the burgers. Dollop a tablespoon of the sauce on top, then brush it over. Flip the burgers again, just for a few seconds – this just very slightly cooks the sauce and gives it some caramelization. Add the cheese and continue to cook until the cheese has melted, and the burger is cooked through. If you test with a probe thermometer it should reach 72°C.

5. Lightly toast the burger buns and assemble the burgers with salad and your choice of condiments.

Joe's Tip

When adding the BBQ sauce to the burgers, don't brush directly from the pan or bowl holding the sauce just in case it comes into contact with the raw meat. Spoon it on first and then brush.

FREEZE

Fishcakes

One of my dad's favourites. He'd always keep any leftover fish from a fish dinner, and he'd say to Mum, 'I'll do dinner tonight; I'll make some fishcakes'. I like making fishcakes with a nice bit of cod or haddock and I use plenty of fish and cut down on the mash, so they're good and healthy. Sometimes I replace some of the regular fish with 200g of so of what the kids call 'yellowfish' – smoked haddock – which makes them extra tasty.

Makes 8 Fishcakes

250g floury potatoes such as
   Maris Pipers or King Edwards,
   peeled and cut into chunks
600g cod or haddock fillet,
   skinned
2 spring onions, very finely
   chopped
zest of 1 lemon
½ small bunch of dill, finely
   chopped
2 tbsp plain flour
2 eggs
75g breadcrumbs
vegetable oil, for frying
salt and black pepper

TARTAR SAUCE
200g mayonnaise
½ small bunch of dill, finely
   chopped
1 tbsp finely chopped tarragon
   leaves
3 tbsp finely chopped capers
1 gherkin or 4 cornichons, finely
   chopped
1 tbsp lemon juice

1. First make the mash. Put the potatoes in a pan of cold water, bring to the boil and cook for about 15 minutes or until tender. Drain and mash, then season with salt and pepper and leave to cool.

2. Put the fish fillets in a single layer in a large frying pan that has a lid. Sprinkle them with salt and cover the fish with water. Bring to the boil, then put the lid on the pan and remove the pan from the heat. Leave it to stand for 5 minutes, then drain off the water. The fish should be just cooked through. When it's cool enough to handle, flake the flesh and remove any bones.

3. Put the fish in a bowl and add the cooled mashed potato, spring onions, lemon zest and dill. Season with plenty of salt and pepper and mix thoroughly. The mixture should hold together well. Divide it into 8 portions and shape into patties.

4. Put the flour, one of the eggs and half the breadcrumbs in separate shallow bowls. Dust each fishcake in the flour and pat off any excess. Dip it in the egg and make sure it is completely coated, then dip it in the breadcrumbs. Continue coating the rest of the fishcakes and when you have used up the first lot of egg and breadcrumbs, add the rest – this way they don't get too messy.

5. If you have time, put the fishcakes in the fridge to chill for at least 30 minutes so they firm up and are easier to cook.

6. To make the tartar sauce, mix all the ingredients together with a pinch of salt and some freshly ground black pepper.

7. To cook the fishcakes, pour a thin layer of oil over the base of a large frying pan. Heat until medium–hot, then add the fishcakes. Fry them for a few minutes on each side until well browned and piping hot all the way through. Check by inserting the tip of a knife or skewer into a fishcake – it should feel too hot to touch for more than a second or two. Drain the fishcakes on kitchen paper, then serve with the tartar sauce.

FREEZE

Turkey Meatballs
with Spaghetti

Turkey is cheap and healthy and makes great meatballs. You might be surprised to see cinnamon in the sauce ingredients. You don't notice the flavour, but it adds sweetness to the sauce so you're less likely to need any sugar.

Serves 4

MEATBALLS

500g turkey (or chicken) mince
100g fresh breadcrumbs
2 tsp garlic powder
1 tsp dried oregano
1 tbsp tomato purée
25g Parmesan cheese, grated
1 egg
salt and black pepper

TOMATO SAUCE

2 tbsp olive oil
1 large onion, finely chopped
4 garlic cloves, finely chopped or crushed
2 tsp dried oregano
¼ tsp ground cinnamon
2 x 400g tins chopped tomatoes
2 sprigs of basil, plus extra to garnish
sugar (optional)

TO SERVE

400g spaghetti or linguine
grated Parmesan cheese
garlic bread (see page 266)

1. Start with the tomato sauce. Heat the olive oil in a large saucepan and add the onion. Cook over a gentle heat until the onion is very soft and translucent but don't let it take on any colour. Add the garlic and cook for another couple of minutes.

2. Stir in the oregano and cinnamon, then add the tomatoes. Swill out the tins with a little water (about 200ml in total) and add this to the pan. Season with plenty of salt and pepper. Remove the leaves from the sprigs of basil and add the stems to the pan. They will add flavour as the sauce cooks.

3. Bring to the boil, then turn the heat down and cover the pan with a lid and leave the sauce to simmer for 30 minutes. Remove the lid and continue to simmer the sauce until it has reduced the sauce by about a third. Taste and add more salt or pepper if you think it needs it. You may want to add a little sugar at this stage as well if the tomatoes are very acidic – start with just ½ teaspoon. Roughly tear the basil leaves and add them to the sauce. Fish out the stems and discard.

4. To make the meatballs, put all the ingredients in a large bowl and season with 1 teaspoon of salt and a good grinding of black pepper. Knead the mixture with your hands – messy, but necessary – until you feel the texture change. It will start to firm up a bit as you do so.

5. Divide the mixture into 20 balls. You can weigh them to make sure they are all about the same size if you like or use an ice-cream scoop as a measure. When shaping the balls, it helps to have wet hands as the mixture may be quite sticky.

Continued on the next page

6. Preheat your oven to 200°C/180°C fan/gas 6. Line a baking tray with some baking paper and place the meatballs on it, evenly spaced. Bake them in the oven for 20 minutes until lightly browned, then carefully add them to the tomato sauce. Put the pan of sauce back on the heat and leave it to simmer for a few minutes.

7. While the meatballs and sauce are cooking, bring a large saucepan of water to the boil and add plenty of salt. Add the pasta and cook for about 10–12 minutes or until just al dente – cooked but still with a little bite to it.

8. Drain the pasta – not too thoroughly – and tip it back into the saucepan. Serve the pasta topped with the meatballs and sauce, garnished with torn basil leaves. Sprinkle with grated Parmesan and season with some more black pepper.

Joe's Tip

For a change, we like to eat this in a garlic bread sandwich – spaghetti and all! You won't need as much spaghetti. Open out the garlic bread and squish down the insides so you create a hollow without losing all the garlicky goodness. Ladle a bit of the sauce on both sides, then fill the hollow with spaghetti. Slice the meatballs and add those to the spaghetti. Add plenty of basil leaves, grated Parmesan and black pepper. See page 266 for my garlic bread recipe.

QUICK

Carbonara ...
with added greens

This was one of the first things I learned to make when I was a single dad and cooking for my Harry. I've always loved it and I still make it now – often adding some extra veg to make it a bit healthier. There are lots of stories about how this dish came about, but one of the most likely is that it was invented when the American soldiers were in Rome during the war and missing their bacon and egg breakfasts!

Serves 4

500g spaghetti or linguine
200g peas (fresh or frozen)
100g rocket or spinach
1 tbsp olive oil
150g pancetta or bacon, diced
4 eggs
100g Parmesan, finely grated,
    plus extra to serve
salt and black pepper

1. First bring a large saucepan of water to the boil and add 2 teaspoons of salt. Add the pasta and cook until just al dente – cooked but still with a little bite to it. When it is almost ready (after 10 minutes, test every minute), add the peas and the rocket or spinach, just to heat through and wilt down.

2. While the pasta is cooking, heat the olive oil in a frying pan and fry the pancetta or bacon until crisp. Beat the eggs and Parmesan together in a bowl.

3. Drain the pasta, reserving a couple of ladlefuls of the cooking liquid. Tip the pasta back into the saucepan and leave for a minute to let the steam subside.

4. Pour in the egg and cheese mixture and stir to combine. If the mixture looks as though it is curdling as it cooks in the heat of the pasta, add 75–100ml of the cooking liquid and keep tossing the pasta until the sauce looks smooth.

5. Stir in the bacon or pancetta and serve immediately with plenty of black pepper and more Parmesan grated over the top.

Mac and Cheese

Two of my kids' favourite things in the world are cheese and pasta, so this is the most beautiful combination for them. Sometimes I mix in a pinch of mild curry powder and a little smoked paprika for a bit of extra depth and flavour, but that's up to you. I might add some roughly crushed croutons or breadcrumbs on top for the last 10 minutes to give some extra crunch.

Serves 4-6

500g macaroni
salt and black pepper

INFUSED MILK
750ml milk
3 bay leaves
1 slice of onion
1 mace blade

SAUCE
50g butter
1 onion, finely diced
3 garlic cloves, finely chopped
50g plain flour
1 tsp garlic powder
1 tbsp Dijon mustard
¼ tsp cayenne pepper
150ml single cream or
   evaporated milk
100g Cheddar, grated
100g Gruyère, grated

BACON (OPTIONAL)
1 tbsp olive oil
150g thick-cut smoked
   bacon, diced

TOPPING
50g Cheddar, grated
50g Gruyère, grated
50g mozzarella, grated

1. First put the milk into a saucepan with the bay leaves, onion slice and mace blade. Bring to the boil and remove from the heat. Leave to cool to just above room temperature.

2. Bring a saucepan of water to the boil and add salt. Add the macaroni and cook until al dente, following the packet instructions. Preheat your oven to 200°C/180°C fan/gas 6.

3. Next, make the sauce. Heat the butter in a saucepan and add the onion. Cook over a very gentle heat until the onion is soft and translucent, then add the garlic. Cook for another couple of minutes, then add the flour and garlic powder. Stir until well combined into a paste (roux), then continue to cook, stirring constantly, for 3–4 minutes to cook the flour.

4. Strain the milk. Add a generous splash of it to the roux and stir vigorously – the paste will immediately thicken and come away from the base of the pan. Continue adding the milk, stirring well with each addition, until you've added it all and you have a thick pourable sauce.

5. Add the mustard, cayenne pepper and the cream or evaporated milk and beat until well combined. Remove from the heat and add both cheeses, stirring until it has all melted.

6. When the macaroni is cooked, drain and add it to the sauce. Stir thoroughly to combine – you don't want the macaroni to clump together. If including the bacon, fry it in the oil until crisp and browned. Pile everything into an ovenproof dish and sprinkle with the cheeses.

7. Bake in the preheated oven for about 30 minutes until the cheese is bubbling and browned in patches.

Mac *and* Cheese Arancini

QUICK

ONE-POT

FREEZE

Arancini are an Italian treat usually made with leftover risotto. But some macaroni cheese makes a brilliant version too and my kids love these. Well worth making extra for!

Makes 8

250–280g leftover mac and cheese (see page 138), chilled
25g Parmesan, finely grated
40g plain flour
½ tsp dried oregano
1 egg
dash of hot sauce
100g panko breadcrumbs
25ml olive oil, for brushing
salt

1. Preheat your oven to 200°C/180°C fan/gas 6. Line a baking tray with parchment.

2. Scoop the mac and cheese into balls. The easiest way is to use an ice-cream scoop, which will give you balls weighing 30–35g each. Press each one quite tightly with your hands – you want to try to get rid of some of the air and compress them. If you find they are sticking to your fingers, wet your hands.

3. Put the Parmesan, flour and dried oregano in a bowl and mix thoroughly with a pinch of salt. Break the egg into a separate shallow bowl and beat until smooth. Add the hot sauce.

4. Put half the panko breadcrumbs in a bowl.

5. Dip the balls in the flour mixture, then dust off the excess and drop into the egg. Make sure the balls are well covered, then coat in the breadcrumbs, topping up as necessary.

6. Place them on the baking tray and brush with the oil. Bake in the preheated oven for about 15 minutes until crisp and lightly golden and piping hot.

ONE-POT

Beef Stir-fry

My mum used to do stir-fries for us when we were kids – it was during her experimental period as a cook. We had a wok and everything. Now I like to make them for the family – they're a good way of getting lots of vegetables into the kids. Just make sure all your vegetables are prepped before you start cooking and this is a breeze. I like to cut the steak into thin strips, and I use a technique called velveting which means marinating them in a mixture of cornflour, rice wine and soy sauce. It makes the meat beautifully tender and means you can use a cheaper cut of steak – such as bavette.

Serves 4

400g bavette, flank or skirt steak
2 tbsp cornflour
1 tbsp rice wine
2 tbsp dark or light soy sauce
salt

STIR-FRY
100g dried noodles
½ tsp sesame oil
2 tbsp vegetable oil
1 carrot, cut into strips (peeling optional)
1 red pepper, cut into strips
200g asparagus tips
150g baby corn, cut in half
4 garlic cloves, finely chopped
10g fresh ginger, peeled and cut into matchsticks
1 bunch of spring onions, whites and greens separated, finely sliced
100g beansprouts
1 tsp sesame seeds

SAUCE
2 tbsp dark or light soy sauce
1 tbsp rice wine vinegar
1 tbsp rice wine
1 tsp hot sauce, such as sriracha
½ tsp Chinese 5 spice

1. First prepare the beef. Put the steak between 2 sheets of clingfilm and give it a good bash with a meat tenderizing mallet or a rolling pin. Remove the meat from the clingfilm and cut it into thin strips across the grain. Season with salt.

2. Whisk together the cornflour, rice wine and soy sauce in a bowl. Add the strips of beef and toss to coat. Marinate for at least 30 minutes – or leave it in the fridge overnight if you want to prepare ahead.

3. Mix the sauce ingredients together and set aside. Cook the noodles according to the packet instructions, then drain and toss in the sesame oil to help prevent them sticking together.

4. When you are ready to start cooking, put half the vegetable oil in your wok and heat it until very hot – the air above the oil will look as though it is shimmering slightly, and it will be too hot to hold your hand over for long.

5. Add the beef and stir-fry very briefly just to sear on all sides. Remove and set aside. Wipe the wok out if necessary and add the remaining oil. Heat until hot again.

6. Add the carrot, pepper, asparagus and baby corn. Stir-fry until close to being cooked but still with a bite to them, then add the garlic, ginger and spring onion whites. Cook for another couple of minutes, then put the beef back in the wok.

7. Add the beansprouts and noodles, then pour over the sauce. Continue to stir-fry, turning everything over until the sauce is evenly distributed and it is all piping hot. Serve in warm bowls, garnished with the spring onion greens and sesame seeds.

FREEZE

My **Special Lamb Casserole**

When the money was running low at the end of the week, my mum used to make a dish we called baked bean surprise. It was baked beans with any other oddments of veg or ingredients she had in the fridge and some sliced potatoes on top. When we heard this what was coming, we'd think 'What has she put in it now?'. I like to use this sliced potato topping on my version of a classic French lamb casserole. This brings back good memories.

Serves 6

1kg lamb neck fillet
2 tbsp plain flour
1 tsp mustard powder
1 tsp mixed dried herbs
3 tbsp olive oil
12 button onions or shallots
4 large or 6 medium carrots, cut into chunks (peeling optional)
3 celery sticks, cut into 4cm lengths
4 garlic cloves, finely chopped
250ml red wine
2 tbsp tomato purée
1 tsp apple or redcurrant jelly
250ml lamb or vegetable stock
1 large sprig of rosemary, leaves picked
1 large sprig of thyme
750g floury potatoes, such as Maris Pipers or King Edwards, thinly sliced (peeling optional)
25g butter, melted
salt and black pepper

1. Cut the lamb into fairly large chunks – about 5cm long – and trim off any really hard pieces of fat. Put the flour, mustard powder and dried herbs in a bowl. Season with salt and pepper and mix, then toss the lamb in this seasoned flour.

2. Heat 1 tablespoon of the olive oil in a large frying pan. When it's hot, add the lamb and sear it on all sides until well browned. Set aside. You might need to do this in a couple of batches so that you don't overcrowd the pan.

3. Heat the remaining oil in a large flameproof casserole dish. Add the onions or shallots and carrots and fry over quite a high heat, shaking the casserole dish regularly, until the onions or shallots have taken on some colour. Add the celery and garlic and continue to cook for another 2–3 minutes.

4. Add the lamb to the casserole dish, then pour in the red wine. Bring to the boil and let the wine bubble furiously for a couple of minutes. Stir in the tomato purée and jelly and pour in the stock. Add the herbs and season with salt and pepper.

5. Bring back to the boil, then turn the heat down and cover the casserole dish with a lid. Leave to simmer for 1–1½ hours until the meat is tender.

6. Arrange the sliced potatoes on top and sprinkle with a little more salt. Cover and continue to cook until the potatoes are tender – another 15–20 minutes.

7. Preheat the grill to a medium setting. Brush the potatoes with the melted butter and place the casserole dish under the grill for a few minutes until the potato topping is lightly brown and crisp.

Mediterranean Traybake

A nice veggie supper, this is good served with a big green salad and maybe some couscous or a pile of cooked green beans and new potatoes. It's one of those meals you can put together in the morning and it's ready to put in the oven when everyone's home from work and school.

Serves 4

2 medium red onions, cut
   into wedges
3 peppers (any colour),
   deseeded and cut into
   thick strips
3 courgettes, cut diagonally
   into 2cm rounds
1 tsp dried oregano
3 tbsp olive oil
juice of ½ orange
1 garlic bulb, broken into cloves
1 tsp dried mint
1 x 225–250g block of halloumi,
   cut into 1cm slices
2 tsp balsamic vinegar
12 cherry tomatoes, halved
12 olives, any colour, pitted
   if you like
1 handful of fresh basil leaves
salt and black pepper

1. Preheat your oven to 180°C/160°C fan/gas 4.

2. Put the onions, peppers and courgettes into a large roasting tin. Sprinkle over the oregano and 2 tablespoons of the oil, then pour the orange juice over the veg. Mix thoroughly so the vegetables are well coated with oil and herbs. Add the garlic cloves on top and season with salt and pepper.

3. Roast for 25 minutes, giving the tin a good shake once or twice so nothing catches on the bottom.

4. Mix ½ tablespoon of oil with the mint. Arrange the halloumi slices on top of the vegetables and brush them with the minty oil. Mix the remaining ½ tablespoon of oil with the balsamic vinegar. Add a generous pinch of salt and toss the tomatoes in this mixture. Add the tomatoes, olives and basil leaves to the roasting tin.

5. Roast for another 15–20 minutes or until everything is tender and lightly browned around the edges.

Joe's Tip

Unless you have a really big roasting tin, I find it's best to divide the ingredients for this between 2 tins. If all the veg are too crowded together they tend to steam rather than brown a little.

ONE-POT

Hunters' Chicken Traybake

This is so simple to make and so good. It has a sort of hunters' chicken vibe – like that chicken, bacon and tomato casserole that's popular in Italy and France, but in the form of a traybake. Great served with some cheesy mash or colcannon (see page 261).

Serves 4

3 leeks, sliced into 2–3cm rounds
100g thick bacon lardons
300g squash or pumpkin, unpeeled and cut into wedges
4–8 chicken bone-in thighs (skin on)
2 tbsp olive oil
2 large sprigs of thyme
1 tsp dried sage
400g chestnut mushrooms, halved if large
salt and black pepper

SAUCE

2 tbsp tomato purée
2 tsp Dijon mustard
1 tbsp maple syrup
1–2 tsp hot sauce (smoked, such as chipotle, if possible), or to taste
1 tsp garlic powder
50ml dark or light soy sauce
75ml red wine
2 tsp dried mixed herbs
3 garlic cloves, crushed

1. Preheat your oven to 200°C/180°C fan/gas 6.

2. Arrange the leeks, bacon and squash or pumpkin in a large roasting tin and tuck in the chicken thighs. Drizzle over the olive oil and season with salt and pepper. Add the thyme sprigs and sprinkle over the sage. Roast in the oven for 25 minutes.

3. Meanwhile, make the sauce. Put the tomato purée, mustard, maple syrup and hot sauce in a bowl and add the garlic powder. Whisk this in before adding any liquid – it has a tendency to clump otherwise – then add the soy sauce, red wine, herbs and garlic. Season with a little salt and pepper.

4. Add the mushrooms to the roasting tin, then pour the sauce over and around the contents, making sure you brush some onto the chicken skins.

5. Roast for another 20–25 minutes until the sauce has reduced a little, the chicken is cooked through with a crisp skin and the vegetables are tender.

Joe's Tip

Squash and pumpkin are a bit of a nightmare to peel, so I don't bother. Once it's cooked you can eat the skin if it's tender enough and it's good healthy fibre. Or if you prefer, just scrape off the flesh and leave the skin.

WEEKENDS

Cooking for the family is my passion

We usually have my mum and other family around at the weekend and there's nothing I like better than cooking up a big Sunday dinner for them all. It might be a roast with all the trimmings, but I like to ring the changes too and cook big, tasty pies like my nan Betty used to make, or special dishes like paella or moussaka.

ONE-POT

Seafood Paella

This always reminds me of sunshine, seaside and holidays but I often make it at home too – even when it's raining. We all love a good paella.

Serves 6

24 raw prawns, shells and
heads on
3 tbsp olive oil
400g cleaned squid, cut into
rounds
100ml white wine
1.3 litres fish, vegetable or
chicken stock
200g hot cooking chorizo, cut
into rounds
1 large onion, finely chopped
1 red pepper, finely diced
1 green pepper, finely diced
2 firm courgettes, sliced into
rings
4 garlic cloves, finely chopped
or crushed
1 tbsp smoked paprika
zest and juice of 1 lemon
2 bay leaves
2 tsp dried oregano
4 ripe, medium tomatoes,
puréed
large pinch of saffron, soaked
in 2 tbsp warm water
500g paella rice
300g green beans, cut into
short lengths
100g peas, defrosted
500g cleaned mussels
salt and black pepper
1 lemon, cut into wedges,
to serve

1. First prepare the prawns. Set 6 aside for garnish, then remove the heads and the shells from the rest, leaving just the tips of the tails. Devein, if necessary, by cutting down the centre of the backs and pulling out the black digestive tract.

2. Heat 1 tablespoon of the oil in a large sauté or frying pan or a paella pan if you have one. When hot, add all the prawns and cook them briefly on both sides until they have turned pink. Remove them from the pan and set aside.

3. Now add the rounds of squid and cook until they turn opaque. Remove and set aside.

4. Add another tablespoon of oil to the pan and add the heads and shells of the prawns. Stir-fry until they've turned pink, then add the wine. Bring to the boil and leave it to bubble away for a couple of minutes, then add the stock. Bring back to the boil, then turn the heat down and leave to simmer for 10 minutes. This gets all the lovely prawn flavour into the stock. Strain the stock and set aside.

5. Heat the remaining 1 tablespoon of oil in the pan. Add the chorizo and fry until it has crisped up and rendered out plenty of oil. Remove the chorizo from the pan and set aside. Add the onion and peppers and cook gently until the onion is soft and translucent.

6. Add the courgettes, garlic, paprika, lemon zest and herbs to the pan. Stir for a couple of minutes, then stir in the tomatoes. Add the saffron liquid to the stock. Pour this into the pan and stir to make sure any sticky bits from the bottom of the pan are mixed in. Season generously with salt and pepper.

7. Sprinkle in the rice in an even layer. Top with the green beans, the peas and the cooked squid. Return the chorizo to the pan too.

8. Bring to the boil, then turn the heat down to a simmer and cook for 15 minutes. Add the prawns, including those with the shells on, and the mussels. Continue to cook until the rice is tender, the liquid has been absorbed and the mussels have opened. (Discard any mussels that don't open.) Sprinkle over the lemon juice.

9. Remove from the heat and cover with a lid or a tea towel. Leave to stand for 10 minutes then serve with the lemon wedges.

Caramelized Onion *and* Tomato Tart

I didn't think I could make stuff like tarts before I went on *Celebrity MasterChef* but look at me now! Nadia Sawalha is a good friend, and she was such an amazing support to me when I was on the show. She was my go-to person and I'd phone her up, tell her what I was thinking of making and she'd give me loads of good advice on things like making good pastry. For this tart, make sure you cook the onions for a really long time, so they get all soft and delicious.

Serves 4

1 portion shortcrust pastry
   (see page 264 or 450–500g
   shop-bought pastry)
plain flour, for dusting

FILLING
2 tbsp olive oil
15g butter
3–4 medium onions (about
   500g), finely sliced
1 tbsp sherry vinegar
½ tsp demerara sugar (optional)
3 garlic cloves, finely chopped
1 large sprig of thyme, leaves
   picked, or 1 scant tsp dried
   thyme
2 tbsp Dijon mustard
100g Gruyère or Comté, grated
50g Parmesan, grated
500g mixed tomatoes, thickly
   sliced or halved
salt

1. Preheat your oven to 180°C/160°C fan/gas 4. Put a baking tray into the oven to heat up.

2. Roll out the pastry on a floured surface and use it to line a 25cm round fluted tin. Leave some pastry hanging over the edge as it will shrink a little. Prick the pastry all over with a fork, then place in the fridge to chill for 15 minutes.

3. Cover the pastry with a piece of baking paper (scrunching up the baking paper first helps it sit better), then add some baking beans or dried beans to weigh it down. Place the tin on the heated baking tray and bake for 15 minutes. Remove the beans and paper and bake for another 5 minutes, then remove from the oven and leave to cool.

4. Heat the olive oil and butter in a large frying pan. When the butter has melted and foamed, add the onions and fry them very gently for 30–45 minutes until soft and golden. Add the sherry vinegar and sprinkle with the sugar, if using. Stir until the sugar has dissolved and looks slightly sticky. Stir in the garlic and most of the thyme, then cook for another 2–3 minutes.

5. Cool the onions – the quickest way is to transfer them to a large bowl rather than leaving them in the hot pan. Stir in the mustard and cheeses, making sure that they are evenly distributed and not clumped together. Spoon everything evenly into the pastry case.

6. Arrange the tomatoes on top, keeping them as close together as possible. Brush with oil and sprinkle with salt and more thyme.

7. Bake in the preheated oven for 20–25 minutes until the tomatoes have softened and are lightly browned. Remove from the oven and leave to stand until almost room temperature before serving.

Bacon *and* Broccoli Quiche

My mum used to make quiche for us when we were kids and she'd buy them ready made as well sometimes. It's something my family like and it's all good stuff – eggs and plenty of veg. You can add any cooked vegetables you have so it's great for using up leftovers. I like to make a big one and have it hot for one meal and then some cold the next day for a snack or in a packed lunch.

Serves 6

1 portion of shortcrust pastry
 (see page 264 or 450–500g
 shop-bought pastry)
plain flour, for dusting

FILLING
1 tbsp olive oil
1 small onion, finely chopped
100g bacon, diced
150g broccoli, cut into
 small florets
4 eggs
300ml double cream
100ml milk
50g Cheddar, grated
salt and black pepper

1. Preheat your oven to 180°C/160°C fan/gas 4. Put a baking tray into the oven to heat up.

2. Roll out the pastry on a floured surface and use it to line a 25cm round fluted tin. Leave some pastry hanging over the edge as it will shrink a little. Prick the pastry all over with a fork, then place in the fridge to chill for 15 minutes.

3. Cover the pastry with a piece of baking paper (scrunching up the baking paper first helps it sit better), then add some baking beans or dried beans to weigh it down. Place the tin on the preheated baking tray and bake for 15 minutes. Remove the beans and paper and bake for another 5 minutes, then take the tin from the oven and leave the pastry case to cool.

4. To make the filling, heat the olive oil in a frying pan. Add the onion and fry over a medium–low heat until the onion has softened and looks translucent. Turn up the heat and add the bacon. Fry until the bacon has browned.

5. Bring a pan of water to the boil, add salt and then the broccoli. Cook for 3–5 minutes until it is just tender. Check by inserting the tip of a knife into the stem – if it slides in easily it is done. Drain thoroughly.

6. Crack the eggs into a bowl and season with salt and pepper. Whisk until completely broken down (a uniform yellow/orange), then stir in the cream and milk. Don't whisk at this stage as you don't want the mixture to get frothy.

7. To assemble, spread the onion and bacon over the base of the cooked pastry case. Arrange the broccoli over the top, then pour in the egg and cream mixture. Sprinkle over the cheese.

8. Bake in the oven for 20–25 minutes until the top has browned and the egg mixture has set with a very slight wobble in the centre. Great hot or cold.

Steak *and* Mushroom Pie

The last time I saw my nanny Betty, I asked her to make a steak pie for me, but sadly she died soon after that. I always think of her and her amazing pie skills when I make this. With this, and any pie, be sure to let the filling cool down properly before putting it into the pastry case.

Serves 6

1 portion of shortcrust pastry (see page 264 or 450–500g shop-bought)
plain flour, for dusting
1 egg, beaten, for brushing

FILLING
1 tbsp beef dripping or olive oil
800g stewing or braising steak, trimmed of fat and diced
30g butter
2 onions, finely chopped
4 garlic cloves, finely chopped
2 tbsp plain flour
150ml red wine
1 tbsp tomato purée
1 tsp Worcestershire sauce
400ml beef stock
1 large sprig of thyme
1 bay leaf
400g chestnut mushrooms, quartered
salt and black pepper

1. First make the filling and allow it to completely cool down before using. Heat the beef dripping or olive oil in a large frying pan. Season the steak generously with salt and pepper, then fry until well browned. It's best to do this in a couple of batches so you don't overcrowd the pan – if you try to cook too much at once, the meat will steam and not brown. Set aside.

2. Heat half the butter in a large flameproof casserole dish. Add the onions and cook them over a gentle heat until soft and translucent, stirring regularly. Add half the garlic and cook for 2 minutes. Sprinkle in the flour and stir until it looks like a paste has formed around the onions.

3. Pour in the red wine and continue to stir until well combined with the onions, then stir in the tomato purée. Add the Worcestershire sauce, beef stock and browned steak. Tuck in the herbs and season with salt and pepper. Bring to the boil, then cover the casserole dish with a lid and turn the heat down to a simmer. Cook for about 1 hour or until the beef is tender.

4. Heat the remaining butter in a frying pan. Add the mushrooms and season with salt and pepper. Fry briskly over a medium–high heat until lightly browned, then add the rest of the garlic and continue to cook until any liquid given out by the mushrooms has evaporated.

5. Add the mushrooms to the beef. Remove the casserole dish from the heat and leave the mixture to cool completely.

6. When you are ready to assemble and bake your pie, preheat your oven to 200°C/180°C fan/gas 6.

7. Take two-thirds of the pastry and roll it out on a floured surface to fit your pie dish. Line the dish with the pastry, pile in the filling, then brush the pastry border with beaten egg.

8. Roll out the remaining pastry and use it to form a lid. Trim the pie and crimp the edges together. Brush with beaten egg and cut a couple of slits in the top to allow steam to escape. Bake in the oven for 35–40 minutes until the filling is piping hot and the pastry is crisp and golden brown.

I'm a Celebrity...

Once I knew I was going to be written out of *EastEnders*, my agent started putting the word around that I'd be available for work.

As it happened, we had a family friend, Daisy, who was a casting director on *I'm a Celebrity...Get Me Out of Here!* and she knew before most people that I was leaving *EastEnders*. She asked me if I fancied being in the Jungle. Wow! Definitely!

Everything happened so quickly after that, but I do remember thinking to myself that if I messed this up that would be it. I was about 25 at the time and just a raw young actor. I'd never had any media training or anything. My mum, as always, really encouraged me and told me just to go out there and enjoy myself – and most importantly to be myself. She said it would be the biggest adventure of my life. Her advice really stuck with me, and I remember saying to myself every day when I was out there: just enjoy it, Joe, this is a once in a lifetime experience.

First day out there, I met all the celebs and we had to go into the Jungle for the first time. As I walked into the clearing and saw the little campfire it all looked so beautiful, and I knew immediately I was going to be fine. I just loved it. There were certainly ups and downs and plenty of dramas that year, but I thoroughly enjoyed it all. It was the making of me. And incredibly, I won.

Before I did *I'm a Celebrity...*, I'd signed up to do a panto in Chatham. At that time, of course, I'd no idea I was going to do well in the Jungle, let alone win it. Back then, in 2008, it was before streaming and all that and everyone watched the show. When I came home I found I was famous! I went down to Chatham to start rehearsing for the panto and I remember the high street being full of people all screaming my name. It was such a big deal – like being one of The Beatles. I couldn't believe it.

For the next 10 years, I went back to Australia every year and did the spin-off show. I met all the celebs and was part of that incredible family of people. It was amazing. And of course, I met Stacey. I realize now that getting ill when I did was one of those sliding-doors moments. If I hadn't got ill, I would have stayed on *EastEnders* and I wouldn't have been on *I'm a Celebrity*. And if I hadn't done that, I wouldn't have met Stacey.

In life, I've learned that terrible things might happen but then the bigger picture can be amazing. Life can be like that sometimes.

It was the making of me. And incredibly, I won!

Toad *in the* Hole

My dad loved the good old British classics. He didn't cook that often but when he did, toad in the hole was one of his favourites. It was one of the first dishes I learned to cook and something I still make to this day. My kids love it and I sneak in some leeks for a bit of extra veg.

Serves 4

25g butter
3 leeks, sliced into rounds
1 tbsp olive oil or beef dripping
8 large sausages
salt

BATTER
150g plain flour
2 eggs
275ml whole milk

TO SERVE
onion gravy (page 270)

1. Begin by making the batter. Put the flour in a bowl with a generous pinch of salt and whisk thoroughly to get rid of any lumps.

2. Crack the eggs into the bowl. Using a whisk, gradually work the flour into the eggs until you have a thick paste. Then gradually add the milk to make a smooth thick batter that's about the consistency of double cream. If you prefer, you can make the batter by just putting all the ingredients into a food processor or blender and blitzing. Whichever method you use, leave the batter to stand for 1 hour before using.

3. Now, prepare the leeks. Melt the butter in a frying pan that has a lid. Add the leeks and stir to coat them with the butter. Add a splash of water and a generous pinch of salt, then cover the pan and leave the leeks to cook over a very gentle heat until they are tender.

4. Preheat the oven to 180°C/160°C fan/gas 4. Put the olive oil or beef dripping in a large roasting tin. If using beef dripping, put the tin in the oven for a couple of minutes to melt the fat.

5. Add the sausages to the tin and roll them around in the oil or fat so they are coated all over. Cook them in the oven for 20 minutes, giving them a shake every so often, until browned nicely browned.

6. Add the leeks to the sausages and make sure they are evenly spread over the tin. Turn up the oven to 200°C/180°C fan/gas 6.

7. Pour the batter around the sausages and check again to make sure the sausages are evenly spread out. Put the tin back in the oven and bake for about 30 minutes until the batter is well risen and has turned a rich dark golden brown. Serve with onion gravy (see page 270).

Roast Chicken *with* Stuffing *and* Gravy

When I learned to cook one of my first passions was making a Sunday roast. I love a Sunday roast and pride myself on it. I love producing it for the family. This is my version – my go-to Sunday dinner, with a nice bit of stuffing and some tasty gravy.

Serves 4-6

1 x 1.5–2kg chicken
½ tsp dried mixed herbs
1 onion, thickly sliced
a few sage leaves
25g butter, softened
squeeze of lemon juice
salt and black pepper

STUFFING

15g butter
2 shallots, finely chopped
200g mushrooms, finely chopped
2 garlic cloves, finely chopped
4 large fresh sage leaves, finely chopped
zest of ½ lemon
130g sausage meat or 2 sausages
25g fresh or dried breadcrumbs

GRAVY

2 shallots, finely chopped
50g bacon lardons (optional)
100ml red wine
400ml chicken stock
2 bay leaves
2 tsp cornflour

1. If you have bought your chicken a day or two in advance of cooking it, remove all the packaging, put it on a plate and sprinkle it with salt and the mixed herbs. Wrap it loosely in kitchen paper and put in the fridge, making sure nothing else is touching it. This really makes a difference to the crispness of the skin.

2. Remove the chicken from the fridge an hour before you are ready to roast it, so it can come up to room temperature. Preheat your oven to 220°C/200°C fan/gas 7.

3. To make the stuffing, melt the butter in a frying pan. Add the shallots and mushrooms and fry them over a low–medium heat until the shallots are translucent and the mushrooms have browned. Any liquid in the pan from the mushrooms should evaporate away.

4. Stir in the garlic, sage leaves and lemon zest. Cook for another couple of minutes, then transfer to a bowl to cool. Break up the sausage meat or, if using sausages, remove the skins and break up the meat. Add the sausage meat and breadcrumbs to the mushroom mixture and mix thoroughly – it should clump together well. Season with plenty of salt and pepper.

5. Spoon the stuffing into the chicken – there should be just enough to fill the cavity. Weigh the chicken at this point. Put the onion slices in the middle of a roasting tin. Add the sage leaves. Put the chicken on top and pat it dry with kitchen paper to remove any moisture on the skin. Smear the butter all over the skin and squeeze over some lemon juice. Add 200ml of water to the tin.

6. Put the chicken in the oven and roast for 15 minutes, then reduce the temperature to 180°C/ 160°C fan/gas 4. Cook for 20 minutes for every 500g. So if your chicken weighs 1.5kg, cook for 1 hour.

7.   Check to see if it is done. If you have a probe or meat thermometer, the meat in the thickest part of the thigh and the centre of the stuffing should reach 74°C. If you don't have a thermometer, insert a skewer into the thickest part of the thigh for a few seconds. Remove and touch it – if it is too hot to hold for more than 2–3 seconds, the chicken will be done. You should also see clear liquid coming out of the thigh where you have pierced it. Finally, give chicken the legs a wiggle – if they feel loose – as though they could easily be pulled away, the chicken is ready.

8.   Transfer the chicken and onion to a warm dish and cover with foil.

9.   To make the gravy, drain off any liquid from the roasting tin into a small saucepan. Add the shallots and bacon, if using, to the roasting tin and place over medium–high heat. Fry until the bacon has crisped up a bit, then pour in the red wine. Allow the wine to bubble up, then stir to deglaze the tin. Your aim is to have the base of the roasting tin completely clean. Pour everything from the tin into the saucepan with the roasting juices, then add the stock and bay leaves. Bring to the boil and simmer for several minutes.

10. Mix the cornflour with 2 tablespoons of water and stir until you have a smooth paste. Add this to the gravy and stir until the gravy has thickened slightly. Transfer to a gravy boat or jug and serve with the chicken, stuffing, roast potatoes (see page 258) and any other sides you like.

FREEZE

Chicken *and* Leek Pie

Chicken pie was a favourite of my nanny Betty, who made the best pies. It's one of my best-loved dishes too and I love the combo of chicken and leeks, with a little touch of tarragon.

Serves 6

1 portion shortcrust pastry
  (see page 264 or 450–500g
  shop-bought)
plain flour, for dusting
1 egg, beaten

FILLING
600g chicken thighs, skinned
  and filleted
2 bay leaves
3 sprigs of tarragon
100ml white wine
chicken stock (see method)
50g butter
4 leeks, cut into rounds
3 garlic cloves, finely chopped
50g plain flour
100ml double cream or
  crème fraîche
1 tbsp olive oil
400g mushrooms, halved or
  quartered if large
salt and black pepper

1. First poach the chicken. Put the chicken pieces in a single layer in a saucepan. Season with salt and pepper, then add the bay leaves and a sprig of tarragon. Pour over the wine and just enough water to cover. Bring to the boil, then turn the heat down to a low simmer and cover the pan. Cook for 5 minutes, then remove the pan from the heat and leave to cool.

2. Remove the chicken from the cooking liquor and dice. Pour the liquor into a jug and make it up to 600ml with chicken stock.

3. Melt the butter in a sauté or frying pan that has a lid and add the leeks. Stir until glossy, then add the garlic and a sprig of tarragon. Put the lid on the pan and leave the leeks to braise gently for 10–15 minutes until tender. Remove the tarragon sprig.

4. Add the flour and stir until a paste (roux) develops around the leeks. Continue to cook for 2–3 minutes to cook out the raw flavour of the flour. Gradually add all the cooking liquor/chicken stock mixture, stirring with each addition, until the sauce is the texture of thick cream. Stir in the chicken and the cream or crème fraîche. Finely chop the remaining tarragon sprig and stir that in.

5. Heat the olive oil in a frying pan and add the mushrooms. Season with salt and fry over a medium–high heat until lightly browned. When they look quite dry, remove the pan from the heat and stir the mushrooms into the chicken mixture. Leave to cool.

6. When you are ready to assemble and bake your pie, preheat your oven to 200°C/180°C fan/gas 6. Roll out two-thirds of the pastry on a floured work surface and use it to line your pie dish. Brush the edges with beaten egg.

7. Pile in the cooled filling. Roll out the remaining pastry dough and use it to cover the pie. Trim and crimp the edges together. Brush with beaten egg and cut a couple of slits in the top to allow steam to escape.

8. Bake in the preheated oven for 35–40 minutes until the pastry is golden brown and the filling is piping hot.

Twice-Baked Cheese Soufflés

I learned how to make soufflés when I was on *Celebrity MasterChef* and I remember thinking how on earth I was going to do it – I'd heard they were so hard. But it was the week Tom Kerridge came in and he gave me some tips, so I managed to get one in the oven. I remember sitting there watching the soufflé growing and with every centimetre it grew I just felt so proud of myself. This twice-baked version is slightly different and great because you can get them all ready in advance, then reheat at the last minute.

Serves 4

INFUSED MILK

125ml milk

125ml single cream

2 slices of onion

2 bay leaves

2 cloves

1 garlic clove, finely sliced

SOUFFLÉ

25g butter, plus extra for greasing

15g Parmesan, finely grated

25g plain flour

1 tsp Dijon or tarragon mustard

55g Gruyère or Comté, grated

55g Cheddar, grated

2 eggs, separated

1. Generously butter the insides of 4 x 150ml ramekins, then sprinkle in some of the Parmesan, making sure all of the butter is covered. Shake out any excess.

2. Put the milk and cream in a small saucepan with the onion, bay leaves, cloves and garlic. Bring to just under the boil, then remove from the heat and leave to infuse until room temperature.

3. Preheat your oven to 170°C/150°C fan/gas 3–4. Put the butter in a saucepan. When it has melted, add the flour and stir for 3–4 minutes until you have a paste (roux), allowing some of the raw flavour of the flour to cook out.

4. Strain the milk mixture and gradually add it to the roux, whisking between each addition to make sure there are no lumps. When you have incorporated all the liquid, beat in the mustard. Reserve a tablespoon of each of the cheeses. Add the rest to the pan, then take off the heat and keep stirring until you have a smooth sauce.

5. Beat in the 2 egg yolks. Whisk the egg whites to the soft peak stage. Add a heaped tablespoon to the cheese mixture to loosen it, then carefully fold in the rest, so as not to knock the air out.

6. Divide the mixture between the 4 prepared ramekins and place them in a roasting tin. Pour just-boiled water around them so it comes 1–2cm up the sides of the ramekins. Put the tin in the oven and bake the soufflés for 15–20 minutes until well risen and lightly browned. Leave them to cool (they will collapse down a little), then turn them out and store in the fridge until needed.

7. To reheat, sprinkle with the reserved cheese. Preheat your oven to 180°C/160°C fan/gas 4. Cook the soufflés in an ovenproof dish for 10–15 minutes until piping hot. Pour double cream or tomato sauce around them and sprinkle with more cheese, if you like.

FREEZE

Moussaka

This is my version of the traditional Greek favourite, and it is a real crowd-pleaser – big and hearty and full of flavour. I bulk the lamb mince out with some lentils, and no one notices the difference.

Serves 6-8

MEAT SAUCE

1 tbsp olive oil
1 large red onion, finely chopped
400g lamb mince
3 garlic cloves, finely chopped
1 tsp dried oregano
1 tsp dried mint
1 tsp ground cinnamon
250g cooked brown, green or
  Puy lentils
200ml red wine
400g tin chopped tomatoes
salt and pepper

VEGETABLES

3 aubergines, sliced into
  5mm rounds
3 red peppers, halved and
  deseeded, or a jar/tub of
  roasted red peppers
50ml olive oil
500g floury potatoes, such as
  Maris Pipers or King Edwards,
  thinly sliced

BÉCHAMEL SAUCE

600ml milk
2 bay leaves
1 slice of onion
50g butter
50g plain flour
15g Parmesan, grated
2 egg yolks
grating of nutmeg

1. First make the meat sauce. Heat the olive oil in a large flameproof casserole dish and add the onion and lamb mince. Cook over a medium–high heat for several minutes until the lamb has browned and the vegetables have started to soften.

2. Stir in the garlic, herbs and cinnamon and cook for another 2 minutes. Add the lentils, red wine and tomatoes. Season with salt and pepper.

3. Bring to the boil, then turn down to simmer. Leave the sauce to cook, uncovered, for about 30 minutes until it has reduced down to a thick sauce, stirring every so often.

4. While the sauce is cooking, prepare the vegetables. Preheat your oven to 200°C/180°C fan/gas 6. Brush 2 or 3 baking trays with a little olive oil and arrange the aubergine slices and halved red peppers over them. Brush with olive oil and sprinkle with salt and pepper. Roast in the oven for about 25 minutes until dappled brown and slightly squishy. Remove. Leave the aubergines to cool. Put the peppers in a bowl and cover until they are cool enough to handle, then peel off the skins.

5. Put the potato slices in a steamer over a pan of simmering water and cook for about 10 minutes or until just cooked through.

6. To make the béchamel sauce, put the milk in a small saucepan with the bay leaves and onion and bring to the boil. Remove the pan from the heat and set aside while you make the roux so the onion and bay can infuse the milk with flavour.

7. Melt the butter in a medium saucepan. Add the flour and stir until they are well combined. Continue to cook and stir for a couple of minutes to get rid of the raw taste of flour, then start adding the milk. Add a little at a time, stirring or whisking thoroughly between each addition so the mixture does not go lumpy. When all the milk is stirred in, add the Parmesan. When the cheese has melted, remove the pan from the heat and beat in the egg yolks. Add seasoning and a fine grating of nutmeg.

Continued on the next page

8. When you are ready to put the moussaka together, preheat your oven to 200°C/180°C fan/gas 6.

9. Put about a third of the meat sauce into the base of a large ovenproof dish (measuring at least 30 x 20cm). Arrange half the potatoes, peppers and aubergines over the top in single layers, then pour over the rest of the meat sauce. Add the remaining potatoes, peppers and aubergines in layers. Pour over the béchamel, making sure it completely covers the vegetables.

10. Bake for 25–30 minutes until the top is a patchy golden brown and the sauce is bubbling around the edges. Make sure the moussaka is piping hot all the way through. Leave to stand for a few minutes before serving.

Joe's Tip

For a change, I sometimes like to use courgettes instead of aubergines in my moussaka. Get fairly large courgettes and cut them into slices up to 1cm thick on the diagonal – try to make the slices quite long. Put them on a baking tray, brush with olive oil and sprinkle with salt and pepper, then roast in the oven (200°C/180°C fan/gas 6) for about 20 minutes. Leave to cool, then use in the same way as the aubergines in the recipe.

Fish Pie

Another favourite of my dad's. His mum made the best pies, and he particularly loved a good fish pie. He was a big fan of fish and ate it a lot – he was very health conscious – used to run every day and do half marathons. I like to add a bit of cheese to the sauce, as it just ups the flavour without making it taste cheesy.

Serves 6-8

500g white fish fillets, such as cod or haddock, skinned
250g smoked haddock fillet, skinned
200g shelled prawns
200g scallops, sliced (optional)
2 bay leaves
600ml milk
salt and black pepper

SAUCE
50g butter
1 leek, finely chopped
50g plain flour
100ml white wine
50g Cheddar, grated
1 small bunch of dill, finely chopped

TOPPING
1kg floury potatoes, such as Maris Pipers or King Edwards, peeled
25g butter, plus extra for dotting on top
100ml milk

1. Season the fish, prawns and scallops, if using, with salt and pepper. Put them in a saucepan and add the bay leaves and milk. Slowly bring to the boil, then cover the pan with a lid and remove it from the heat. Leave to stand – the fish and seafood will cook in the milk as it cools, and the milk will be flavoured by the fish.

2. Strain the fish and seafood from the milk and break the fillets into pieces, checking for any bones as you go. Pour the milk and bay leaves into a jug.

3. Cut the potatoes into chunks, put them in a pan and cover with cold water. Bring to the boil and season with plenty of salt. Simmer until just tender – about 15 minutes – then drain. Mash thoroughly, then beat in the butter and milk.

4. While the potatoes are cooking, start the sauce. Melt the butter in a saucepan and add the leeks. Stir until they are glossy with the butter. Put a lid on the pan and leave over a low heat for a few minutes, stirring regularly, until tender.

5. Add the flour and stir until it has soaked up all the butter and created a paste around the leeks. Add the white wine and stir until you have a thicker paste and the whole mixture comes away from the base of the pan. Gradually add the milk, making sure you stir or whisk between each addition so the sauce remains lump free.

6. When you have added all the milk, stir in the Cheddar and let it melt. Then add the cooked fish and seafood and the dill. Taste for seasoning and add salt and pepper if necessary.

7. Pour the mixture into a large ovenproof dish and leave to cool. Preheat your oven to 200°C/180°C fan/gas 6.

8. Spread the mashed potato over the filling and rough it up with a fork. Dot with butter. Bake in the oven for 20–25 minutes until the potatoes are dappled brown, everything is piping hot and the filling is trying to burst through the mashed potato round the edges. Leave to stand for 5 minutes before serving.

FREEZE

Slow-Roast Lamb

This North African-inspired recipe brings back great memories of a trip to Morocco a couple of years ago, filming with *This Morning*. It was the first time I'd been somewhere and seen such a vivid culture change. I remember going to the market and it was alive with colours and smells and noise. It was like an overdose to my senses – one of the most amazing awe-inspiring experiences – and I've never felt an atmosphere like that anywhere else.

Serves 4-6

1 shoulder of lamb, on the bone
4 garlic cloves, thinly sliced
a few sprigs of rosemary
2 tbsp olive oil
zest and juice of 1 lemon
1 tbsp ras el hanout
1 large pinch of saffron threads
2 onions, thickly sliced
a few garlic cloves, unpeeled
500ml chicken or vegetable
  stock
75g soft dried apricots
salt and black pepper

COUSCOUS
200g couscous
½ tsp dried mint
½ tsp mixed dried herbs
1 tbsp olive oil
juice of 1 orange
200ml tepid water
2 spring onions, finely sliced
seeds from ½ pomegranate
25g flaked almonds, toasted
fresh mint leaves

1. Cut slits all over the lamb and insert slices of garlic and half the rosemary sprigs. Mix the olive oil with the lemon zest and juice, the ras el hanout and the saffron threads. Add salt and pepper and rub this mixture all over the lamb. Leave in the fridge to marinate for a couple of hours or overnight if possible.

2. Remove the lamb from the fridge 45 minutes–1 hour before you want to start roasting it. Preheat your oven to 220°C/200°C fan/ gas 7.

3. Put the onions, garlic and remaining rosemary in a large roasting tin and set the lamb on top. Pour in the stock. Place in the preheated oven and roast for 30 minutes. Turn down the heat to 150°C/130°C fan/gas 2 and cook for 2 hours.

4. Remove from the oven and tuck the apricots under the lamb. Put it back in the oven and cook for another 1–2 hours until tender. Start checking after 1 hour – if the bone feels loose when you pull it, it will be just about ready. The meat should be tender and close to falling off the bone.

5. Put the lamb on a warm serving dish with the onions and apricots. Strain off the liquid from the pan. Leave it to cool for a few minutes and take off any fat that settles on top. Squeeze the flesh out of the garlic and whisk into the liquid. Reheat and serve as a gravy.

6. Put the couscous in a bowl and add the dried mint and mixed herbs along with plenty of seasoning. Drizzle in the olive oil and pour over the orange juice. Add the tepid water and cover the bowl. Leave to stand for 5 minutes or until all the liquid has been absorbed.

7. Fluff up the couscous with a fork, then garnish with the spring onions, pomegranate seeds, almonds and mint leaves. Serve with the lamb.

Cola-Glazed Ham

I got invited to a cooking workshop in Marbella with Jean-Christophe Novelli when I was in *EastEnders*, and I took my mum along. One of the things he did was glazed pork belly with cola and it worked really well. My mum tried it, but she forgot to remove the nipples from the belly and my sister got one in her mouth – never again! The cola glaze is great with a nice piece of ham though, and I like to add some cherries too to make it extra special. Good one at Christmas.

Serves 6-8

1 x 2kg ham
up to 2 litres of cola
1 onion
a few cloves
a few allspice berries
a few black peppercorns
2 bay leaves

GLAZE

1 tbsp Dijon or wholegrain
   mustard
1 tbsp soft light brown sugar

SAUCE (OPTIONAL)

15g butter
1 shallot, finely chopped
1 sprig of thyme, leaves picked
50ml port or red wine
1 tsp soft light brown sugar
1 tsp red wine vinegar
100ml cooking liquor
200g black cherries (frozen or
   from a jar)
1 tsp cornflour (optional)

1. First check whether the ham needs soaking or not. It will usually say so on the packaging if you've bought it from a supermarket. Alternatively, ask your butcher. If it does need soaking, put it in a large saucepan, cover with cold water and bring to the boil. Drain and chuck away the water, then rinse out the saucepan and give the ham a rinse too if it has any white foamy starch on it. Check the weight of your ham so you can work out the cooking time.

2. Put the ham back in the saucepan. Add just enough cola to cover it. Stud the onion with a few cloves, then add the allspice berries, peppercorns and the bay leaves to the saucepan.

3. Bring to the boil, then cover the pan and turn the heat down to a simmer. Leave to cook for 1 hour per kg, then remove from the heat and leave the ham to cool in the cooking liquor.

4. Remove the ham and put it on a chopping board. Cut off any string and remove the skin, making sure you leave a thin layer of fat behind. Take a sharp knife and score a diamond pattern all over the area where you have removed the skin, making sure you cut just a little into the flesh. Stick cloves in the corners of the diamonds.

5. Preheat your oven to 220°C/200°C fan/gas 7. Mix the glaze ingredients together, then brush all over the ham. Line a roasting tin with baking paper or foil and place the ham on top. Roast in the oven for about 20 minutes or until the glaze has darkened.

6. To make the sauce, heat the butter in a small pan. Add the shallot and cook gently until soft and translucent. Add the thyme leaves and port or red wine and bring to the boil, then stir in the sugar, vinegar, ham cooking liquor and the cherries. Simmer until the cherries are tender. If you want to thicken the sauce, whisk the cornflour with a little water and stir into the cherries. Heat gently, stirring constantly until the sauce has thickened. Serve with thick slices of the ham.

Let's
CELEBRATE

Family, food
and togetherness
- that's what I love

My idea of a great celebration involves plenty of great food. So, when we have a special occasion, I like to make a proper feast and the three ideas in this chapter are my favourites. I'll get in the kitchen and cook up a storm, then load the table up with as many delicious dishes as I can. Everyone can then dig in and help themselves.

Indian Feast

When it's takeaway night, the Solomons always go for an Indian, so I decided to have a go at making some Indian favourites myself. A great way to get some brownie points with the family and the kids all love it. I've mastered the art of onion bhajis, samosas and kofte and I make a mean chicken korma. I serve it all up with huge bowlfuls of pilau rice, raita and Stacey's favourite, mango chutney.

Serves 4-6, depending on how many dishes you make

Onion Bhajis

I like to make my batter with a mix of gram flour and cornflour, which makes for lovely crisp bhajis. The nigella seeds work well, but you could use cumin seeds instead or just leave them out.

2 medium onions, finely sliced
70g gram (chickpea) flour
30g cornflour
1 tsp baking powder
1 tsp garlic powder
1 tsp curry powder of your choice
½ tsp ground turmeric
½ tsp chilli flakes or 2 green
  chillies, finely chopped
½ tsp nigella seeds (optional)
1 tbsp Greek yoghurt
up to 100ml water
vegetable oil
salt

1. Put the onions in a bowl and sprinkle 1 teaspoon of salt over them. Cover with cold water and leave to stand for 30 minutes.

2. Put both flours into a bowl with the baking powder, garlic powder and spices. Season with salt and whisk to remove any lumps. Add the yoghurt and enough water (up to 100ml) to make a batter with a thickness similar to double cream.

3. Drain the onions and pat them dry with a tea towel or on kitchen paper. Add them to the batter.

4. Half-fill a deep-fat fryer or large saucepan with oil. Heat it to about 180°C – if you drop in a tiny piece of onion it should immediately bubble around the edges.

5. Drop heaped tablespoons of the batter-coated onion into the hot oil, a few at a time. Don't overcrowd the pan – if you do the temperature of the oil will drop and your bhajis will not be crisp. Fry for 2–3 minutes on each side until a deep yellow/orange.

6. Drain the bhajis on kitchen paper and serve while crisp and piping hot. Serve with raita (see page 195).

FREEZE

Vegetable Samosas

You can make nice samosas with just peas and potatoes, but I prefer to pack some more veggies in there for lots of flavour.

Makes 16

300g potatoes, peeled and diced
1 tbsp coconut or olive oil
1 tsp mustard seeds
1 tsp cumin seeds
1 onion, finely chopped
1 small courgette, diced
1 carrot, peeled and coarsely grated
5g fresh ginger, peeled and finely chopped
3 garlic cloves, finely chopped
1 tbsp curry powder
100g frozen peas
salt

TO ASSEMBLE
5–6 sheets of filo pastry
½ tsp ground turmeric
75ml butter, melted, or olive oil
1 tsp nigella or sesame seeds

1. Put the potatoes in a saucepan and cover with freshly boiled water. Add plenty of salt and bring to the boil. Simmer for 3–4 minutes until just tender. Drain and put them in a bowl.

2. Heat the oil in a large frying pan and add the mustard seeds and cumin seeds. When they start to pop, add the onion, courgette and carrot. Cook gently for a few minutes until the onion is translucent.

3. Stir in the ginger and garlic and cook for another couple of minutes, then add the curry powder.

4. Add the contents of the frying pan to the potatoes and stir, trying not to break up the potatoes too much. Add the frozen peas – their temperature will help cool down the potatoes and vegetables. Leave the mixture to cool completely and transfer to the fridge to chill until needed.

5. When you are ready to assemble the samosas, remove the filling from the fridge. Cut your filo pastry into long strips measuring about 30 x 10cm. Cover them with a damp tea towel so they don't dry out.

6. Whisk the turmeric into the melted butter or oil and brush it all over a strip of filo. Place the filo with one of the short edges nearest you. Take a heaped tablespoon of the filling and put it at the bottom of the strip. Take the bottom corner and fold it diagonally over the filling to the opposite edge, so it forms a triangle. Press down along the cut edges of the triangle, then keep folding up until you run out of pastry. Press gently along the samosa to seal and to even out the filling, then place on a baking tray. Repeat with the remaining filo and filling.

7. To bake, preheat your oven to 170°C/190°C fan/gas 3–4. Brush the samosas with a little more of the butter or oil and sprinkle with the seeds. Bake in the oven for about 20 minutes until crisp and brown.

ONE-POT

FREEZE

Lamb Koftes

My kids love these and they like helping to make them too – shaping the meat around the skewers is lots of fun. The key to success is getting the mixture nice and smooth.

Makse 12 long koftes*

*or 24 torpedo-shaped ones

1 small onion, roughly chopped
3 garlic cloves, roughly chopped
10g fresh ginger, peeled and grated
2 green chillies, deseeded if you prefer, roughly chopped
2 tsp ground cumin
½ tsp ground cinnamon
½ tsp ground turmeric
2 tbsp tomato purée
800g lamb mince
salt and black pepper

12 skewers, soaked for 30 minutes if wood or bamboo

1. Put the onion, garlic, ginger and chillies in a food processor and process until well broken down. Add the remaining ingredients and season with plenty of salt and pepper.

2. Process until the meat has a much finer texture and everything is well combined. Chill for 30 minutes.

3. Line a couple of baking trays with baking paper or foil. Divide the mixture into 12 and form it into long sausage shapes around the skewers. Place them on the baking trays. If you prefer, you could make 24 torpedo-shaped koftes.

4. Grill the koftes in a griddle pan over a medium–high heat for a few minutes, turning them regularly.

5. Preheat the oven to 200°C/180°C fan/gas 6. Place the koftes in the oven until just cooked through with some deep char lines.

6. Alternatively, you can cook them on a barbecue for a few minutes and then transfer to direct heat to develop some charring.

Raita

300ml Greek yoghurt
juice of ½ lime
1 tsp dried mint
½ tsp ground cumin
¼ tsp ground cinnamon
¼ tsp caster sugar
salt

1. Put the yoghurt in a bowl and add all the remaining ingredients with a generous pinch of salt. Stir.

ONE-POT

FREEZE

Pilau Rice

I like the whole spices in this, but if you're feeding young kids, I think it's best to take the spices out before serving.

500g basmati rice
2 tbsp olive oil, butter or
   coconut oil
1 large onion, finely chopped
2 star anise, broken up into
   spokes
6 cardamom pods
4 cloves
3cm cinnamon stick, broken
   into long shards
1 tsp coriander seeds
1 tsp cumin seeds
1 tsp black peppercorns
3 bay leaves
½ tsp ground turmeric
salt

TO GARNISH
green chillies, finely sliced
sprigs of coriander

1. First rinse the rice – this will remove the excess powdery starch which can make it sticky once cooked. Pour the rice into a large bowl and cover with cold water. Swirl around so the water goes cloudy, then pour the water away. Keep doing this until the water becomes clear. Alternatively, you can put the rice in a large sieve and run it under the tap. Drain and set aside.

2. Heat the oil or butter in a large saucepan. Add the onion and sauté over a fairly gentle heat until soft and translucent. Turn up the heat and add all the whole spices and bay leaves. Stir for 2–3 minutes until they give off a strong aroma, then stir in the rice and turmeric.

3. Cover with 1 litre of cold water and bring to the boil. Add plenty of salt – at least 2 teaspoons. Turn down the heat and cover the pan. Leave to simmer for 15–16 minutes by which time the rice should be cooked, and all the water absorbed.

4. Remove from the heat. Cover the saucepan with a tea towel and replace the lid, then leave to stand for 10–15 minutes for perfect, fluffy rice. Turn into a serving dish and garnish with sliced chillies and coriander.

ONE-POT

FREEZE

Easy Chicken Korma

This is a favourite curry in our house and it's really easy to make. Just be sure to allow time to marinate the chicken so it's lovely and tender.

Serves 4-6

700g chicken thigh fillets, diced
1 tbsp coconut oil, ghee or
    vegetable oil
2 onions, finely sliced
4 garlic cloves, crushed or
    grated
25g fresh ginger, peeled and
    grated
1 tbsp spice mix (see page
    273), mild curry powder or
    ½ tsp each ground cinnamon,
    cardamom, coriander,
    turmeric, fenugreek, plus
    a pinch of cloves
1 small tomato, puréed
100g ground almonds
100ml double cream or yoghurt
salt and black pepper

MARINADE
zest and juice of 1 lime
1 green chilli
1 garlic clove
2 tsp spice mix (see page 273)
    or mild curry powder

TO GARNISH
sliced green chillies
coriander

1. First, marinate the chicken. Put it into a bowl and season with plenty of salt and pepper. Add the lime zest. Put the chilli and garlic in a small food processor with a splash of water and blend until quite smooth. Add this to chicken with the spice mix and lime juice. Mix thoroughly, cover and leave to stand for at least 1 hour, or overnight if possible.

2. When you are ready to make the curry, heat the oil or ghee in a large flameproof casserole dish. Add the onion and cook gently until soft and translucent. Add the garlic and ginger and continue to cook for another 2 minutes, then add the chicken.

3. Cook the chicken over quite a high heat until coloured, then sprinkle in the spice mix, curry powder or spices. Stir until it no longer looks powdery, then stir in the tomato and ground almonds.

4. Season with salt and pepper, then add 250ml of water. Bring to the boil, then turn down the heat and leave to simmer, uncovered, for about 15 minutes or until the chicken is cooked through and the sauce has reduced.

5. Stir in the double cream or yoghurt and leave to simmer very gently for a few minutes. Don't let the sauce boil as it is likely to split. Serve garnished with green chillies and coriander sprigs.

Joe's Tip *I like using whole spices as they keep much better than ground and you can always make a big batch, so you aren't forever grinding spices. Try my spice mix on page 273.*

Tomato and Onion Salad

A nice simple little salad is what you need to go with the rest of my Indian feast and this one is full of flavour.

1 red or white onion, finely sliced

400g tomatoes, halved and sliced

zest and juice of 1 lime

¼ tsp caster sugar

½ tsp dried mint

a few sprigs of mint, leaves picked

2 green chillies, finely chopped (optional)

salt

1. Put the onion in a bowl and sprinkle with salt. Cover with water and leave to stand for 30 minutes. This will take away some of the astringency of the onion and make the salad more cooling.

2. Drain the onion and put it in a serving bowl with the tomatoes. Season with more salt and add the lime zest and juice. Sprinkle in the sugar and mint, then toss. Garnish with a few mint leaves and some finely chopped green chilli if you want some heat.

3. Leave to stand at room temperature until you are ready to eat.

Meeting Stacey

When I was in my late twenties I felt like I'd given up on having a proper family life. I'd gone through a hard time with my first big relationship – with my Harry's mum. After we split up, it was so hard not seeing Harry every day.

At that time, I was doing the *I'm a Celebrity...* spin-off show, *Extra Camp*. That time in Australia every year was the light at the end of the tunnel for me and I loved it, but the rest of the time, life wasn't going the way I wanted. I fell into a weird depression and found life really difficult. I'd walk down the street and look at other people and wonder how they got through life so easily. Things sort of stood still for about five years. It got to a point when I would just turn off my phone and disappear. I'd stay in bed for a couple of days. I wouldn't even answer when my mum rang and then she'd be round banging on the door because she'd be worried I'd do something silly. The Jungle was the only bright spot. It was the one thing that made me keep going – somewhere I could go and reinvent myself and be a different person. It saved me for a while.

I got custody of my son and things started to look up. Then in 2015 I met Stacey on a show called *Virtually Famous*. It was about three weeks before I was due to fly out to Australia for the spin-off show and I remember having a laugh with her and encouraging her to come out and be on the programme. It was the first time I'd seen her since she won the Jungle in 2010. So she did come out to Australia and when she saw me she came running over and gave me a big cuddle. From that moment, I knew there was something between us. I just knew. She was out in Oz for four days and we spent all our time together. I thought she was amazing.

The day she was due to leave I thought to myself I've got to do something about this. I've got to let her know how I feel, how amazing I think she is. I sent her a message and asked if I could come over to her room and say goodbye. My plan was that as soon as she opened the door, I was going to kiss her and see what happened. So she opened the door and I threw myself at her and started kissing her – but it was like kissing a wall! She wasn't kissing me back! Then she pulled away. I just wished her a safe flight home and left. What had I done?

I knew
we were
going to
be together
forever!

But when she got home we phoned each other every night for the three or four weeks I was still out there. We really got to know each other – it was like courtship by Skype. I spoke to her family too and got to know them.

Stacey had said to come over when I got home to England and say hello. I went to her place straight from the airport, jetlagged after a long flight and a bit all over the place. She opened the door and omigod the whole family was there – her mum, her dad, cousins. There were about 15 members of the Solomon family in the house. I nearly had a nervous breakdown, but we knew we had something. We knew we were going to be together.

Surf *and* Turf Feast

I've loved my time working in Australia and I love the way they celebrate Christmas. So, my surf and turf feast is how I imagine I would celebrate Christmas on the beach in Australia – and it tastes just as nice in Essex. This features our favourite shrimp, calamari and steak, all cooked on the barbecue, plus a big salad and best of all – my famous triple-cooked chips (page 260).

Serves 4-6, depending on how many dishes you make

Grilled Prawns

Ready-peeled prawns are fine for this recipe, but it's a good idea to check them over and remove any bits of black digestive tract from the centre of the bodies.

18–24 large peeled, headless prawns
lime wedges, for serving
salt and black pepper

MARINADE

2 garlic cloves, crushed
1 red or green chilli, finely chopped
zest and juice of 1 lemon or lime
2 tbsp olive oil

GARLIC MAYONNAISE

2 egg yolks
2 garlic cloves, crushed
½ tsp garlic powder
pinch of curry powder (optional)
1 tsp Dijon mustard
300ml sunflower, rapeseed or groundnut oil
squeeze of lemon or lime juice

4–6 skewers, soaked for 30 minutes if wood or bamboo

1. First marinate the prawns. Put the garlic, chilli, lemon or lime zest and juice and olive oil in a bowl and whisk in plenty of salt and pepper. Add the prawns and stir to coat. Put in the fridge for at least 30 minutes.

2. Make the mayonnaise. Put the egg yolks in a bowl with the garlic, garlic powder, curry powder, if using, the mustard and a generous pinch of salt. Whisk until well combined.

3. Drizzle in the oil, just a very few drops at a time to start with, whisking constantly until the mixture thickens. When it is clear that everything is combining nicely, you can start drizzling in the oil at a steadier rate but keep it fairly slow. Keep going until you have added all the oil. If it starts to look too oily – as if it is about to split – add a few drops of hot water and whisk thoroughly to get the mayonnaise back on track before continuing with the oil.

4. Whisk in a squeeze of lemon or lime juice and taste, then add more salt, pepper and juice as you like. Cover the bowl and store in the fridge – give the mayo another quick whisk before serving.

5. When you are ready to grill the prawns, thread them onto the skewers. Arrange the skewers of shrimp directly over the hot coals and cook for 2–3 minutes on each side until pink and starting to char. Serve with lime wedges and garlic mayonnaise.

Grilled Calamari

Squid, or calamari, is a big favourite with my family. Sometimes we deep-fry squid rings, but the easiest option is to cook pieces of squid on the barbecue. Super-quick and full of flavour.

600g squid tubes
zest of 1 lemon
1 tsp dried oregano
1 tsp sweet smoked paprika
   (optional)
2 tbsp olive oil
salt and black pepper

TO DRESS
juice of 1 lemon
a few chilli flakes
1 small bunch of mint, leaves
   picked

1. First prepare the squid. Cut cut down one side of the tube so it can be opened up and laid flat, then cut into 4 pieces. Make sure there are no sharp pieces of quill attached and trim off any cartilage. Repeat with all the squid tubes.

2. Pat the pieces dry and place them outer-side down. Score a deep criss-cross pattern on the inside of each piece of squid, making sure you don't cut right the way through.

3. Put the lemon zest and dried oregano in a bowl with the paprika, if using, and olive oil. Whisk together and add plenty of salt and black pepper. Add the squid and leave to marinate in the fridge until you are ready to cook.

4. Grill on the barbecue over direct heat for 2–3 minutes on each side until cooked through and slightly charred. The flesh will turn a matte white under the oil and pieces will turn in on themselves. Remove from the barbecue and dress with the lemon juice, chilli flakes and mint leaves.

Joe's Tip

You can also cook the squid on a griddle pan. Heat the pan until it is too hot to hold your hand over, then grill the squid for 3–4 minutes on each side – it will take slightly longer than on the barbecue, as your pan is likely to be not quite as hot.

Barbecued Steak

When barbecuing steak, I find it easier – and cheaper – to cook one big piece instead of separate portions. Always give the steak time to rest before slicing.

1 x 600–800g piece rump steak, 3–4cm thick
2 tbsp olive oil
salt and black pepper

1. Remove the steak from the fridge at least 30 minutes (preferably 1 hour) before you want to cook it. Remove any packaging and lightly cover with kitchen paper.

2. Just before you start grilling, rub the meat with the olive oil and season with plenty of salt and pepper.

3. Cook over a medium–high heat, ideally turning just once, until it is cooked to your liking and well charred. For a steak this thick, it will need 2½–3½ minutes per side for rare, 4–5 minutes for medium rare to medium and 5½–6½ minutes on each side for well done.

4. When it is cooked to your liking, remove and lightly cover with foil. Leave to rest for at least 5 minutes, preferably 10, then slice and pile onto a platter. Season with a little more salt and pepper before serving.

QUICK

ONE-POT

Summer Salad

Have the salad ready to go, then grill the spring onions on the barbecue just before serving. It's nice to include a good mixture of herbs and salad leaves so every mouthful tastes a little different.

100g mixed salad leaves, preferably including rocket and watercress
½ large cucumber, diced
100g radishes, sliced into rounds
250g cooked beetroot, diced
250g cherry tomatoes, halved
1 small fennel bulb, finely diced
2 oranges, skin cut away and sliced into rounds
1 bunch of spring onions, trimmed
200g feta, cubed (optional)
a mixture of herbs to serve – mint, dill, basil, cress, microherbs

DRESSING
4 tbsp olive oil
juice of 1 lemon
1 tsp sherry vinegar
1 tsp Dijon mustard
½ tsp honey
pinch of medium curry powder
1 garlic clove, sliced in half
salt and black pepper

1. First make the dressing. Whisk everything together and season with plenty of salt and pepper. Leave the garlic in there just to infuse and give a hint of flavour to the dressing.

2. Arrange the salad leaves over a large platter and top with the cucumber, radishes, beetroot, cherry tomatoes, fennel and orange.

3. Grill the spring onions on the barbecue for just 1–2 minutes on each side – they will quickly take on char lines and soften. Alternatively, heat a griddle pan and cook them for 3–4 minutes on each side. Cut into 2cm rounds and add to the salad, along with the feta, if using.

4. Drizzle over the dressing, discarding the garlic, and top with a good mixture of herbs.

Mexican Feast

I love a feast and my favourite way of eating and socializing with the family is to get all the food on the table and let them dig in and help themselves. My kids' favourite is a Mexican feast and they love to get involved with mashing avocado, rolling up tortillas and snacking on nachos. This is a great combination of dishes – something for everyone and there's even a burrito to make with any leftovers.

Serves 4-6, depending on how many dishes you make

Nachos *with* Soured Cream

These are a nice little starter for everyone to nibble on before the rest of the meal is ready. They're really good, so don't make too many or everyone will fill themselves up!

150–170g bag nachos
3 tbsp pickled jalapeños
3 spring onions, sliced into rounds
100g Cheddar, grated
50g stretchy cheese, such as mozzarella, or something stronger like raclette if preferred, grated

DIP
200g soured cream
zest and juice of ½ lime
1 tsp garlic or onion powder
¼ tsp chipotle powder, or smoked paprika for less heat
salt

1. Preheat your oven to 200°C/180°C fan/gas 6. Spread the nachos over the base of a roasting tin. Sprinkle over the jalapeños and spring onions, then top with the cheese.

2. Bake in the oven for 12–15 minutes until the cheese has melted and started to brown in places.

3. While the nachos are baking, mix the soured cream, lime zest and juice and garlic or onion powder together and season with salt. Sprinkle over the chipotle powder or smoked paprika.

4. To serve, either drizzle the soured cream mixture over the nachos straight from the oven or use it as a dip.

ONE-POT

FREEZE

Turkey Chilli

I always like to make loads of this, so hopefully there are leftovers for some breakfast burritos the next day!

2 tbsp olive oil
2 medium red onions, diced
1 red pepper, diced
1 green pepper, diced
2 celery sticks, diced
600g turkey mince
4 garlic cloves, finely chopped
1 tbsp chipotle paste
2 tsp dried oregano
1 tbsp ground cumin
1 tsp ground coriander
½ tsp ground cinnamon
½ tsp ground allspice
2 bay leaves
400g tin chopped tomatoes
2 x 400g tins pinto, red kidney
   or black beans, drained
400ml chicken stock
salt and black pepper

TO SERVE
guacamole (see below)
salad (see page 212)
rice
corn tortillas, warmed,
   or taco shells
grated cheese
lime wedges
coriander sprigs

1. Heat the olive oil in a large saucepan. Add the onions, peppers and celery. Cook over a medium heat until the vegetables have started to soften around the edges and the onion has turned translucent.

2. Turn up the heat and add the turkey mince. Cook, stirring regularly, until all the meat has browned. Reduce the heat again to medium and add the garlic cloves. Cook for another couple of minutes.

3. Stir in the chipotle paste, then sprinkle in the oregano and spices. Add the bay leaves, then pour in the tomatoes, beans and stock. Season with salt and pepper.

4. Bring everything to the boil, then turn down the heat and partially cover the pan with a lid. Simmer for about 1 hour, stirring every so often to make sure the chilli isn't catching on the base of the pan.

Guacamole

No Mexican meal is complete without avocado, spiced up with a bit of lime.

juice of 1 lime
3 avocados, peeled and stoned
½ tsp smoked or hot paprika
salt

1. Put the lime juice into a bowl with a generous pinch of salt. Add the avocados and mash. The consistency can be as you like – smooth through to chunky. Sprinkle with smoked or hot paprika.

Leftover Breakfast Burritos

Adding some eggs and bacon is a great way to use up any leftover chilli, but you could also make the burritos part of your feast.

Makes 2 burritos

1 tbsp olive oil

4 slices of smoked streaky bacon, chopped

200g leftover chilli or chilli and rice (see page 215)

knob of butter

2 eggs, beaten

2 large tortillas

50g cheese, grated

leftover guacamole (see page 215) and or soured cream

hot sauce or tomato sauce

1 tbsp leftover salad or spring onions, finely chopped

salt and black pepper

1. Heat the olive oil in a frying pan. Add the bacon and fry until cooked through, then add the leftover chilli or chilli and rice and stir until heated through.

2. In a separate pan, melt the butter. Season the eggs and add them to the pan. Cook, stirring constantly, until scrambled.

3. To assemble each burrito, heat each tortilla on a dry frying pan, just to soften them slightly so they are easier to fold.

4. Divide the bacon/chilli combo in half and pile in a strip down the centre of each tortilla. Top with grated cheese and any guacamole or soured cream. Drizzle over some hot sauce or tomato sauce and spoon over the leftover salad or spring onions. Add the scrambled egg.

5. Fold up the burritos. Fold over the short edges (usually the top and bottom), then fold over one of the longer sides, then roll until you have a rectangular parcel.

6. Wrap in foil to keep warm and to make them easier to hold while eating. Alternatively, cut in half and serve on a plate.

Chopped Salad

Serve this salad with the turkey chilli and guacamole – but save enough to add to your breakfast burritos.

1 red onion, finely chopped

juice of ½ lime

6 medium tomatoes, finely chopped

1 large romaine or cos lettuce, finely shredded

1 tsp dried oregano

1 tbsp olive oil

salt

1. Put the red onion in a large bowl and sprinkle with salt. Pour over the lime juice and toss. Leave to stand for 30 minutes – this will help brighten up the colour and remove some of the astringency.

2. Just before you are ready to serve, add the tomatoes, lettuce, oregano and olive oil. Toss gently together.

PUDDINGS, BAKES *and* CAKES

Cooking is fun - and a great way to bond with my kids

I'm not much of a pudding man myself but I do enjoy cooking them for the family. The kids love helping me make things like my meringue burgers and DIY trifles. And what I think is that if they are going to eat sweet things, better the treats we make at home, as they are a lot healthier than the bought stuff.

Strawberry Meringue Burgers

Meringues weren't something I'd ever eaten much, or cooked. But a couple of months into our relationship, Stacey asked me to come up to Wales to meet her nan. She kept telling me about her nan's meringues and how amazing they were – crunchy on the outside and chewy in the middle. Stacey was right – they were incredible, and her nan gave me the recipe. I started making them for the kids and came up with the idea of putting my own Joe twist on them – meringue burgers!

Makes 8 Burgers

MERINGUES
3 egg whites, at room temperature
¼ tsp cream of tartar
165g golden caster sugar
10g flaked almonds, finely chopped (optional)

BUTTERCREAM
75g unsalted butter
150g icing sugar
1 tbsp milk
2 tbsp Greek yoghurt (optional)
a few drops of vanilla extract
1 tbsp freeze-dried strawberries, finely chopped (optional)

TO SERVE
8 large strawberries or equivalent

1. Preheat your oven to 150°C/130°C fan/ gas 2 and line 2 baking trays with baking paper. If you want to be very precise with your meringues, use a cookie cutter to mark out 16 x 7cm rounds on your paper to use as a guide, making sure they are at least 3cm apart.

2. Make sure your egg whites are at room temperature. Put them in a bowl with the cream of tartar and whip to the stiff peak stage – at this point the egg whites will look quite dry and they will stick firmly to the base of the bowl, even when you turn it upside down.

3. Whisk the sugar into the egg whites a quarter at a time. You will end up with a very stiff, glossy meringue. Spoon this evenly onto the baking paper – each round should be a heaped tablespoon of meringue and measure about 7cm in diameter. Sprinkle half of the meringues with the finely chopped flaked almonds, if using.

4. Bake in the oven for 45 minutes–1 hour until the meringues are crisp on top and set underneath. Leave in the switched-off oven to cool down very slowly, with the door slightly ajar. This will help them dry out and stop them cooling too quickly.

5. To make the buttercream filling, put the butter in a bowl and beat with an electric whisk until very soft. Add the icing sugar a couple of tablespoons at a time until incorporated, then beat in the milk, the yoghurt, if using, and the vanilla extract. Continue to beat until well combined. Fold in the freeze-dried strawberries, if using. If you have included the yoghurt, chill for 30 minutes.

6. To assemble, swirl some of the buttercream onto a meringue shell. Slice a large strawberry and arrange over the top, making sure it will be visible from the edge. Put a small amount of buttercream on another meringue shell to act as glue and gently hold them together. Repeat to make the rest.

Madeira Cake

My mum used to love making a nice Madeira cake. I didn't like it as kid but learned to love it as I grew up. It was one of those things I thought I couldn't cook – out of my comfort zone – but it's actually way easier than you think.

Makes 10 slices

250g unsalted butter, softened
zest of 1 lemon
200g golden caster sugar, plus
  2 tbsp for sprinkling
200g self-raising flour
100g plain flour
pinch of salt
½ tsp vanilla extract
3 eggs
2 tbsp milk or lemon juice

1. Preheat your oven to 170°C/150°C fan/gas 3–4. Line a large loaf tin with baking paper.

2. Put the butter, lemon zest and 200g of sugar into a bowl and beat with electric beaters until very soft and fluffy.

3. Mix the flours together with a generous pinch of salt. Whisk lightly to remove any lumps.

4. Add the vanilla extract and the first egg to 2 tablespoons of the flour mixture. Fold in until completely combined, then repeat with the remaining eggs and more flour. Fold in the remaining flour, then the milk or lemon juice. The texture of the cake batter should still be fairly firm.

5. Scrape into the prepared tin and smooth the top gently with a palette knife. Sprinkle over the 2 tablespoons of caster sugar.

6. Bake in the preheated oven for about 1 hour. The cake should be a rich golden brown and have shrunk slightly away from the sides. It may also have a crack down the centre, which is quite traditional with a Madeira cake.

7. Leave in the tin for a few minutes, then transfer to a wire rack to cool completely. Store in an airtight tin for up to a week.

Joe's Tip

If you want to vary the flavour, try any citrus fruit such as lime, mandarin and orange. Grapefruit juice works well, too. You can also add other extras such as poppy seeds with lemon juice or chocolate chips with orange.

Yule Log

When I was little, I was easily put off some foods by the name – I didn't like the idea of cheesecake or mince pies. They didn't sound right to me. But a yule log had everything I liked – sponge, chocolate, cream. I'd eat that. We always used to go to my nanny Betty's on Christmas Eve, and it was almost as exciting as Christmas. There'd be a big party and some presents and she'd do loads of food, including yule log. We used to love it and I make it now to bring back those great memories.

Makes 12 slices

HONEYCOMB (OR USE READY-MADE – I LIKE CRUNCHIE BARS)
oil, for greaisng
175g caster sugar
50g golden syrup
25g honey
pinch of salt
1 tsp bicarbonate of soda

GANACHE ICING
300ml double cream
150g dark chocolate, broken up
100g milk chocolate, broken up

SPONGE
oil, for greasing
4 large eggs, separated
100g caster sugar
50g self-raising flour
35g cocoa powder

FILLING
200ml double cream
75g honeycomb
4 tbsp jam (black or sour cherry, or apricot)

TO DECORATE
shards of honeycomb
any Christmassy decorations, such as edible gold stars

1. First get the honeycomb started, if making your own. Lightly oil a shallow, 1-litre dish and line it with baking paper. Put the sugar, golden syrup and honey in a medium saucepan with a pinch of salt and 50ml of water.

2. Slowly heat until everything has dissolved, then continue to cook, stirring regularly, until the mixture has turned a rich golden brown – it should read 149–150°C on a thermometer.

3. Remove the pan from the heat and whisk in the bicarbonate of soda. Be prepared for it to foam up. Quickly pour it into your prepared dish. Do not touch it once you have poured it out, as this might make it deflate. Leave to cool and harden for at least 2 hours. Break up into large chunks or shards.

4. Next, make the ganache. Put the cream and chocolate in a heatproof bowl and place it over a pan of simmering water. Heat, stirring regularly, until the chocolate has completely melted and combined with the cream – it should start to thicken. Pour into a container and leave to cool. Transfer to the fridge to chill.

5. For the sponge, grease a 33 x 23cm Swiss roll tin with a little oil and line it with baking paper. Preheat your oven to 180°C/160°C fan/gas 4.

6. Put the egg yolks and sugar in a bowl and whisk until the mixture is thick and foamy. You should be able to make a trail across the surface with the whisk and it will hold for a few seconds. In a separate bowl, whisk the egg whites to the stiff peak stage.

7. Sieve the flour and cocoa together into the egg yolk and sugar mixture. Carefully fold them in until you have no streaks, and the mixture is a deep brown. Take a couple of spoonfuls of the egg whites and fold them into the mixture to help loosen it a bit, then add the remainder and gently fold in until there are no streaks.

8. Scrape the batter into the prepared tin and smooth over the top to make sure it is even. Bake in the oven for 8–10 minutes, checking after 8 minutes. Be careful not to overcook as if the sponge dries out it will be harder to roll.

9. Remove from the oven. Carefully remove the cake from the tin and upturn it onto a fresh piece of baking paper. Peel off the paper from the underside of the cake. Cover with a tea towel and leave to stand for 5 minutes.

10. Roll up the cake, still in the baking paper. It rolls better while still a little warm and it will be less likely to crack when you re-roll later.

11. Whisk the cream for the filling until thick and quite stiff. Stir in the honeycomb.

12. Unroll the sponge and spread it with jam. Add the cream, spreading as evenly as you can – this is best done with a palette knife. Roll up the sponge again, making sure it isn't so tight that the cream oozes out.

13. Remove the ganache from the fridge. If it is still very soft, put it in the freezer for 5–10 minutes, then beat to loosen it up a bit. Spread it over the sponge, then chill. Remove from the fridge and make lines along the logs with a cocktail stick or tip of a knife to make it look like bark. Add shards of honeycomb and any other decorations you like.

Joe's Tip

The recipe for honeycomb makes more than needed for this recipe but it keeps for ages in an airtight container – and is delicious dipped in melted chocolate!

Looking
back

People talk about love at first sight, and I really think that's how it was for me and Stacey. I've talked about meeting her on *Virtually Famous* in 2015, but some years before we had crossed paths in Australia when she won *I'm a Celebrity*.

I was out there doing the spin-off show and I watched her over those weeks as she won everyone's hearts. Everyone loved her. She was beautiful, funny, sexy – everything. I remember thinking, 'This girl is amazing.' But I was not in a good place with my life, so the idea of getting together with her didn't come up. I just admired her from afar.

I always used to do the first interview with the winner after they came out of the Jungle. I remember seeing her walk across that bridge and it was like something out of a movie – her hair blowing in the wind, sun rising behind her. I thought how fantastic she was, the Queen of the Jungle. What a star. I was so excited. There was this amazing woman coming across the bridge, and I was imagining her smelling heavenly, like roses.

Then she came towards me, I smelled her and whoa! Of all the celebs I interviewed during my time on the show, she was up there in the top five worst smelling – really. I've never smelled anything like it – after all that time in the Jungle, she really stank! Then before I knew it, she was gone, back to England.

I didn't meet her again until years later. It was weird now I think of it that we didn't bump into each other before, but fate works in strange ways. When she won *I'm a Celebrity*... in 2010 our lives were on different paths. But when we did finally meet properly years later, we were ready, both recovered from previous relationships and in a better place with our lives. We felt the same about things. We had the same moral compass. It was meant to be. It just felt like it was meant to be.

She was beautiful, funny and sexy!

White Chocolate Soufflés
with Raspberry Sauce

Getting to grips with making soufflés on *Celebrity MasterChef* was a real stepping stone for me as a cook. I went from thinking that such things were impossible to finding out I could do it. It was an eye-opener, making me realize I could cook really good food if I just put my mind to it and concentrated.

Makes 4

50g caster sugar
30g plain flour
1 tsp cornflour
100g white chocolate, grated
  or chopped
175ml whole milk
3 pieces of pared orange zest
  (optional)
a few drops of vanilla extract
4 eggs, separated
½ tsp cream of tartar (optional)

TO COAT THE RAMEKINS
15g butter, melted
2 tsp caster sugar

SAUCE
250g raspberries (frozen
  are fine)
25g caster sugar
squeeze of lemon juice
½ tsp cornflour (optional)
1 tbsp framboise (optional)

TO SERVE
a few more berries
  (preferably fresh)
200ml double cream (optional)
vanilla ice cream (optional)

1. First make the sauce. Put the raspberries, sugar and lemon juice in a saucepan with 50ml of water. Heat slowly, stirring until the sugar has dissolved, then continue to cook until the raspberries have broken down.

2. If using the cornflour to thicken, mix it with a splash of water. Stir into the berries and keep stirring until the sauce starts to thicken. Push through a sieve into a clean saucepan and add the framboise, if using.

3. You need 4 x 150ml ramekins. To prepare them, brush melted butter around the insides. Dust the insides with caster sugar and put the ramekins in the fridge to chill.

4. Mix the sugar, flour, cornflour and white chocolate together in a medium bowl.

5. Heat the milk with the pared orange zest, if using, and the vanilla extract. When the milk is close to boiling point, pour it from a height over the flour mixture, whisking as you do so. Keep whisking until the chocolate has melted and you have a lump-free liquid.

6. Tip the mixture back into the saucepan and heat, bringing it back up to boiling point. Stir constantly as the custard mixture will thicken very quickly. As soon as you can tell it is thickening, whisk vigorously to prevent any lumps forming.

7. Remove the pan from the heat and transfer the custard to a bowl. Leave to cool, then leave in the fridge to chill for at least half an hour or until you are close to wanting to cook your soufflés.

Continued on the next page

8. Preheat the oven to 200°C/180°C fan/gas 6. Remove the custard from the fridge and beat in the egg yolks.

9. Whisk the egg whites with the cream of tartar, if using, to stiff peaks stage. Fold into the custard mixture, a third at a time. Be gentle, so you don't knock all the air out of the whites.

10. Ladle the mixture into the prepared ramekins right to the top. For the best rise, scrape a palette knife cleanly across the top, then run your finger around the inside rim of each ramekin.

11. Put the dishes in a roasting tin and carefully pour just-boiled water around them. Bake in the oven for 12–15 minutes, until well risen and lightly browned on top. Do not open the oven door to check during this time, as it will cause the soufflés to collapse!

12. Transfer the ramekins to 4 plates or shallow bowls. Pass the raspberry sauce and berries round – it is traditional to break into the top of the soufflé and pour in the sauce and/or cream or ice cream.

Joe's Tip

The cream of tartar isn't essential, but it does help the egg whites rise and stay stable, so worth adding if you have some.

Tottenham Cake

I didn't enjoy school – I wasn't academic at all – but primary school wasn't so bad. We used to have Tottenham cake for pudding at lunchtime and there'd be custard in mad colours. Loved that.

Makes 16-20 slices

250g unsalted butter, softened, plus extra for greasing
250g self-raising flour
2 tsp baking powder
pinch of salt
250g caster sugar
4 eggs
2 tsp vanilla extract
up to 50ml milk
150g raspberries (optional)

ICING

75g raspberries (frozen work best)
250g icing sugar

TO DECORATE

hundreds and thousands

Joe's Tip

I sometimes use those freeze-dried raspberry bits to sprinkle on top instead of hundreds and thousands. Looks really pretty.

1. Preheat your oven to 180°C/160°C fan/gas 4. Grease a 30 x 20cm rectangular tin with butter and line it with baking paper.

2. Put the flour and baking powder into a bowl with a generous pinch of salt and whisk together to get rid of any lumps.

3. Put the butter and sugar into a bowl and beat with electric beaters until very soft, pale and fluffy – it will have increased in volume a lot. You can do this in a stand mixer if you have one.

4. Add the eggs one at a time, with a couple of tablespoons of the flour mixture, mixing between each addition until you have added them all. Add any remaining flour, then stir in the vanilla extract. Add the milk a tablespoon at a time until you have a dropping consistency – this means that the mixture will fall quite easily off a spoon.

5. Scrape the mixture into the prepared tin and smooth over the top with a spatula. If using the raspberries, sprinkle them on top and press them in very lightly.

6. Bake in the preheated oven for about 25 minutes or until the cake is lightly golden brown, springy to touch and has very slightly shrunk away from the sides. Leave to cool in the tin.

7. To make the icing, put the raspberries in a small saucepan with 2 tablespoons of water. Heat gently until the raspberries collapse, then press them through a sieve into a small jug.

8. Sieve the icing sugar into a bowl. Add the raspberry juice a tablespoon at a time until you have a bright, pourable pink icing. Don't add too much at once as you want to make sure the icing isn't too thin – it needs to be the texture that will run very slowly off a spoon.

9. When the cake is cool, pour over the icing. Sprinkle with the hundreds and thousands and leave the icing to set. Remove the cake from the tin, peel off the baking paper and cut into squares.

Chocolate *and* Ricotta Profiteroles

Like soufflés, profiteroles are one of those things that need a bit of practice. The first few times I couldn't get the right consistency – it was too thin, too thick – a Goldilocks situation. But now I've got the knack they're no trouble and a real crowd-pleaser, very impressive and this passion fruit filling is a winner.

Makes 12

PROFITEROLES
75g plain flour
pinch of salt
60g butter
1 tbsp caster sugar
2 eggs, beaten

FILLING
150ml double cream
300g ricotta
50g icing sugar
4 large passion fruit

CHOCOLATE SAUCE
200ml double cream
150g dark chocolate, broken up

1. Preheat your oven to 200°C/180°C fan/gas 6. Line a baking tray with baking paper and dampen it so it sits flat on the tray.

2. Sieve the flour onto a piece of baking paper and add a pinch of salt.

3. Put the butter, sugar and 150ml of water into a saucepan and bring it to the boil. Remove from the heat. Create a funnel effect with the baking paper and pour the flour straight onto the melted butter mixture. Stir vigorously until you have a smooth paste which pulls away cleanly from the base of the pan. It will still be steaming at this stage.

4. Leave to cool for 5 minutes, then gradually beat in the eggs, a little at a time until you have a glossy dough with a slow dropping consistency. This requires elbow grease – you can transfer the mixture to a stand mixer, if you have one, and use the paddle beater.

5. Drop 12 spoonfuls of the dough onto the prepared baking tray, keeping them well spaced out. Wet a finger and lightly smooth down the tops, getting rid of any peaks and curls. Bake in the preheated oven for 18–20 minutes until puffed up and well browned.

6. Remove from the oven. Cut a small slit in the side of each profiterole to allow steam to escape, then put them back in the oven for another couple of minutes. Remove and leave to cool.

Continued on the next page

7. To make the filling, pour the cream into a bowl and whisk until stiff. In a separate bowl, beat the ricotta with the icing sugar. Add the passion fruit flesh to the ricotta, then fold in the cream. Chill for 30 minutes.

8. Spoon the filling into a piping bag. Make a small hole in the base of each profiterole, then pipe in the filling.

9. To make the chocolate sauce, put the cream and chocolate in a saucepan and melt very gently together, stirring regularly until you have a runny sauce. This will thicken as it cools but will liquefy again as soon as it is gently heated. Serve the profiteroles with the chocolate sauce poured over the top.

Joe's Tip

These are best not made too far ahead eating because once they are filled the pastry will start to get soggy. But you can get all elements ready in advance. Keep the filling in the fridge until just before you are ready to serve and gently reheat the chocolate sauce.

Jelly *and* Ice Cream

When I was a kid, you always had jelly and ice cream at a party. It was the go-to party food. But it isn't so common any more – my kids hadn't really had this much til I started making it for them. They love it now – a little blast from my past.

Serves 4-6

JELLY

zest and juice of 6 limes
100g white caster sugar
4 leaves of gelatine
425g tinned pineapple chunks (optional)
vegetable oil, for greasing

ICE-CREAM

3 large ripe bananas
juice of ½ lime
¼ tsp ground cinnamon
1 tbsp caster sugar
1 tbsp honey or maple syrup
75ml double cream

1. For the ice cream, line a baking tray with baking paper. Peel the bananas and cut them into chunks, then toss with the lime juice and cinnamon. Put them in a single layer on the baking tray and place in the freezer. They will take at least 3 hours to freeze solid but are better left overnight.

2. Put the lime zest and juice into a saucepan with the sugar and 100ml of water. Heat slowly until the sugar has dissolved, then leave at a slow simmer for 5 minutes.

3. Meanwhile, break up the leaves of gelatine, put them in a saucer and cover with cold water. When the gelatine has softened, wring it out and add to the lime mixture in the pan. Stir until it has dissolved.

4. Strain the contents of the saucepan through a fine sieve into a jug. Make up the amount of liquid to 500ml with either juice from the tin of pineapple (do not use fresh pineapple juice!) or water.

5. Pour the liquid into lightly oiled jelly moulds or a glass serving bowl. Add the pineapple chunks, if using, and leave to cool. Stir before putting in the fridge to set and chill.

6. When you are ready to make the ice cream, put the frozen bananas in a food processor with the sugar and the honey or maple syrup and the cream. Process until the bananas have broken down and combined with the cream to make thick, smooth ice cream.

7. Eat immediately with the jelly or transfer to a freezer-proof container. If you refreeze the ice cream, remove it from the freezer and transfer to the fridge 30 minutes before you want to eat it.

Joe's Tip

If you want the jelly to be really bright green, add a tiny drop of green food colouring.

DIY Trifles

QUICK

ONE-POT

I'm not much of a pudding fan myself but this is something I love making with the kids and it's a big favourite. Stacey doesn't like it because the kitchen looks like a bomb's hit it once we've finished, but she knows it's fun and good bonding, so worth it. I learned about cooking at a young age, and I think it's important, so I always enjoy getting my kids involved in the kitchen.

Serves 4

500g mixed berries, such as strawberries, raspberries, blueberries, blackberries

1 tbsp caster sugar

50ml elderflower cordial (optional)

squeeze of lemon juice

4 slices of Madeira cake or similar (see page 226 for homemade)

your favourite jam, for spreading

8 amaretti biscuits, crumbled

2 peaches or nectarines, cut into wedges (peeling optional)

200ml custard (see page 278 for homemade, or shop-bought)

300ml double cream or squirty cream

1 tbsp icing sugar

TO DECORATE

flaked almonds, lightly toasted

hundreds and thousands

chocolate curls or flakes

jelly sweets

1. First prepare the fruit. Put the berries in a saucepan with the caster sugar, 75ml of water and the elderflower cordial, if using. Add the lemon juice. Heat gently until some of the berries burst and are sitting in plenty of juice. Strain the fruit, reserving the juice, and leave to cool.

2. Spread two of the slices of Madeira cake with jam and sandwich with the other two. Cut up these cake sandwiches and squash them into the base of 4 glasses or one large bowl. Gently break up the amaretti biscuits and add those too.

3. Pour the reserved fruit juice over the sponge and biscuits, then divide the berries between the glasses. Add the peaches or nectarines.

4. Top with custard. If using double cream, put it in a bowl and whisk until it has reached the soft peak stage. Fold in the icing sugar, then divide between the glasses. Alternatively, squirt over plenty of canned cream.

5. Serve with all the decorations in little bowls for everyone to add as they like.

Blackberry *and* Apple Crumble

My family love a crumble, so I really enjoy making them. Out of pure love I learned how to make a good crumble for them, even though I don't always eat it myself. This one is full of goodness.

Serves 4-6

FILLING

25g butter, plus extra for
  greasing
25g soft light brown sugar
400g eating apples, peeled
  and sliced
1 large Bramley apple, peeled
  and sliced
200g blackberries
½ tsp ground cinnamon

TOPPING

200g plain flour
150g butter, diced
50g porridge oats
75g demerara sugar, plus more
  for sprinkling

1. Preheat your oven to 200°C/180°C fan/gas 6. Butter a 2-litre ovenproof dish.

2. To make the filling, melt the butter in a large frying pan over a medium heat. Add the sugar and stir until it has dissolved. Turn up the heat and add the apples. Cook for 3–4 minutes, shaking the pan regularly. Stir in the blackberries and sprinkle in the cinnamon. Transfer the filling to the prepared dish.

3. For the topping, put the flour into a bowl, add the butter and rub it in with your fingertips. Stir in the porridge oats and sugar. Spread the topping over the filling, making sure you leave it quite loose and not packed down. Sprinkle over another tablespoon of sugar.

4. Bake in the preheated oven for 35–40 minutes until the top is golden and the filling is piping hot – you might see some of it bubble up around the sides.

5. Leave to stand for a few minutes before serving with ice cream, cream or custard.

SIDES and BASICS

I love to get in the kitchen and produce good food

Someone once said to me that if you can master making a few basic things really well, you're on the way to producing great meals. I love potatoes and two of my specialities are roast potatoes and triple-cooked chips. Mine are superb, I promise you! Other basic skills it's good to know are making gravy and proper stock – both can take your cooking to the next level.

Roast Potatoes

I pride myself on my roast potatoes – they change your life! They're one thing that I think I'm the best in the world at making. I'd love for anyone to step up to the plate and give me a roast potato challenge. The secret is in the special mixture I sprinkle on top.

Serves 4

1kg floury potatoes, such as Maris Pipers or King Edwards, peeled and cut into large chunks
1 tbsp cornflour
1 tsp garlic powder
1 tsp dried oregano
1 sprig of rosemary, needles picked and finely chopped
2 tbsp goose fat or coconut oil
salt and black pepper

1. Preheat your oven to 200°C/180°C fan/gas 6.

2. Put the potatoes in a saucepan and just cover with cold water. Bring to the boil and season generously with salt. Return to the boil, then cook for 2 minutes. Drain and tip the potatoes back into the saucepan.

3. Cover the pan with a tea towel and leave to stand off the heat for several minutes to help dry out the potatoes. Mix together the cornflour, garlic powder, dried oregano and rosemary with more salt and a grinding of black pepper.

4. Put the fat or oil in a large roasting tin and place the tin in the oven until smoking hot.

5. Sprinkle the cornflour mixture over the potatoes. Replace the saucepan lid and give the pan a good shake. Remove the roasting tin from the oven and carefully add the potatoes – the fat will be very hot and might splutter. Turn the potatoes over to make sure they are well coated with the fat or oil.

6. Roast in the oven for about 45 minutes, turning every so often until well browned, crisp and with a fluffy inside.

Triple-Cooked Chips

OK, these may sound like a bit of a faff, but I promise you, when you taste them, you'll know it is all worthwhile. People travel miles for my chips. Just be sure to get the oil the right temperature and be careful!

Serves 4

1kg good chipping potatoes, such as Maris Pipers or King Edwards
2–3 litres groundnut oil or 1.5kg dripping, for frying
salt

1. Peel the potatoes and cut into thick chips. Put them in a large bowl and cover with cold water. Swill the water around to remove as much starch as possible, then drain.

2. Put the chips in a steamer basket and sprinkle with salt. Cook over simmering water until they are tender to the point of a knife and starting to crack – about 20 minutes. Remove very carefully, one at a time, from the steamer (tongs work best for this). Pat dry on kitchen paper. If you have time, chill the chips in the fridge until you are ready to cook them.

3. Heat the oil or dripping in a deep-fat fryer or large saucepan, making sure it is no more than two-thirds full. At this stage just heat the oil to 130–150°C, then fry the chips for a few minutes in a couple of batches. You want them to fry to the point they have a crust but haven't taken on any colour – this is part frying.

4. Drain on more kitchen paper. You can get the chips ready up to this point quite far in advance.

5. When you're ready for the final stage, heat the oil to a higher temperature of 180°C. Add the chips – again in a couple of batches – and fry for a couple of minutes until very crisp and a rich brown.

6. Drain on kitchen paper, then sprinkle with plenty of salt and serve immediately, along with malt vinegar and garlic mayonnaise on the side for those who want it.

Joe's Tip

You can boil the chips for the first stage, but I find they keep their shape better and are easier to handle if steamed. Makes life a bit easier. You can prepare this ahead to the last fry, which means you can make a larger batch and they will all be finished quite quickly.

Use dripping for the best flavour but you do need quite a lot of it!

QUICK

Colcannon

We're passionate in our house about potatoes and this is another great way of serving them. Buttery mash with some greens and spring onions mixed in – good for getting some leafy greens into the kids.

Serves 4

1kg floury potatoes, such as
  Maris Pipers or King Edwards
75g butter
1 pointed or small Savoy
  cabbage, shredded
4 spring onions, finely sliced
  (including the greens)
100ml single cream (optional)
salt and black pepper

1. Peel the potatoes and cut them into chunks. Put them in a steamer basket and season with plenty of salt. Steam over simmering water for 15–20 minutes until tender.

2. Melt 25g of the butter in a large sauté pan. Add the cabbage and spring onions and cook gently for a few minutes until they're starting to collapse down and look glossy with butter. Add a splash of water, cover the pan and leave to simmer over a low heat until the veg are tender – another 5 minutes or so.

3. Mash the potatoes – for best results use a potato ricer – and put them in a saucepan. Beat in the remaining 50g of butter, then stir in the cabbage and onion and season with salt and pepper. Add the cream, if using, and stir until well combined. Serve piping hot.

Joe's Tip *Steaming the potatoes gives a much better texture for mashing than boiling. If you do want to boil them, don't peel – the skins will come off easily after cooking.*

Creamed Leeks

I love little side dishes like aioli, garlic mayo and stuff like that. One day I thought I would make something up and I came up with this mix of cream and leeks. Whenever I cook a roast dinner now, I make some of this and everyone dips their roast potatoes in it.

Serves 4

25g butter
4 leeks, sliced into 1cm rounds
1 garlic clove, finely chopped
1 large sprig of thyme
50ml white wine or Vermouth
150ml double cream
salt and black pepper

1. Heat the butter in a large, lidded sauté pan. When it starts to foam, add the leeks and stir to coat. When the leeks look glossy, season with plenty of salt and pepper, then stir in the garlic and thyme.

2. Pour over the wine or Vermouth and cover the pan. Cook the leeks gently over a low–medium heat for about 10 minutes until they are perfectly tender, stirring every so often.

3. Pour in the cream and continue simmering, this time uncovered, until the sauce has reduced down. Serve immediately.

QUICK

FREEZE

Shortcrust Pastry

I always used to buy pastry – and I still do sometimes – but I learned how to make it myself while on *Celebrity MasterChef*. And I have to say, it is better.

Makes 450-500g

300g plain flour
75g unsalted butter, chilled
   and cubed
50g lard, chilled and cubed
   (or another 50g unsalted
   butter)
1 egg yolk
chilled water
salt

1. Put the flour in a bowl and add a generous pinch of salt along with the butter and lard, if using. Rub the fat into the flour until the mixture resembles breadcrumbs.

2. Add the egg yolk and some chilled water, a tablespoon at a time, until the mixture clumps together into a firm dough. One of the keys to really good short pastry is adding as little water as possible but making sure your dough isn't too crumbly.

3. Cover and chill the pastry until you are ready to use it.

Joe's Tip

You can make your pastry in a stand mixer or a food processor if you prefer.

Garlic Bread

There's nothing like the smell of homemade garlic bread! Try making it my way so you can use it to make incredible garlicky sandwiches.

Serves 8

250g butter, softened
10 garlic cloves, crushed
leaves from 3 sprigs of tarragon
  or basil, finely chopped
1 tsp sea salt
35g Parmesan cheese or similar,
  finely grated (optional)
2 long French sticks

1. Preheat your oven to 220°C/200°C fan/gas 7.

2. Put the butter in a bowl and add the garlic, herbs and salt. Mix thoroughly – the butter should be flecked with green and be soft enough to spread. Stir in the grated cheese, if using.

3. Cut the French sticks in half. Next, cut lengthways down one side of each length of bread, making sure you don't cut all the way through. You want to be able to open each length out like a book.

4. Spread both of the cut sides thickly with the garlic butter – the easiest way to do this evenly is by using a palette knife. Close the bread back up, wrap it tightly in foil and place on a baking tray. Repeat with the remaining lengths.

5. Bake for about 15 minutes, then open each foil parcel and put the bread back in oven for another 5 minutes to crisp up. Serve as is or make into sandwiches.

Joe's Tip

This amount of butter will be enough for 2 large French sticks, but if you do have any left over, keep it in the fridge for a few days or freeze it in cubes or logs. You can also freeze the prepared garlic bread. Just cut each length in half, wrap in foil and freeze. They can be cooked straight from frozen but will need about 20 minutes.

ONE-POT

FREEZE

Chicken Stock

I hate throwing food away and I like to use every bit of a chicken when we have one, so using the carcass for stock makes total sense. You can use all the leftovers, including fat and skin, and I sometimes add a couple of chicken wings too for extra flavour. Don't be tempted to make a larger amount with one chicken carcass – the stock will just be weak and watery.

Makes about 1.5 litres

1 chicken carcass, including any fat or skin
2–3 raw chicken wings (optional)
cloves from ½ bulb garlic, unpeeled, plus any papery skin
1 onion, roughly chopped
2 leeks, roughly chopped
2 carrots, unpeeled and roughly chopped
2 tomatoes, roughly chopped
2 bay leaves
2 sprigs of tarragon
1 sprig of thyme

1. Break up the chicken carcass as much as you can and put it in a saucepan with all the remaining ingredients, including the chicken wings, if using. Cover with 2 litres of water and bring to the boil.

2. Turn the heat down to a simmer and start skimming your stock, removing any mushroom-coloured foam. Keep doing this until the foam turns white.

3. Leave to simmer for 2–3 hours, partially covered, until the stock has reduced down to a light golden brown. Strain through a fine sieve and then again through kitchen paper or muslin for extra clarity. Leave to cool.

4. You can skim off any fat before using the stock, but if you are storing it, leave it with a coating of the fat to preserve it. It will keep for up to a week in the fridge or can be frozen for up to 6 months.

Joe's Tip

If you want a richer, darker stock, roast the chicken wings for about 20 minutes in a 200°C / 180°C fan / gas 6 oven before adding them to the pan.

Use any fat you skim off the stock for frying potatoes or onions – it tastes really good.

ONE-POT

FREEZE

Simple Vegetable Stock

I never used to make my own stock, but I've learned what a difference it can make to a dish. Now I try to prepare some regularly and always have some in the freezer. Adding tomatoes and a bit of tomato purée give you a nice rich stock which I like, but if you need a lighter version for some recipes, just leave those ingredients out.

Makes 1.25-1.5 litres

1 tbsp olive oil
1 onion, roughly chopped
2 leeks, roughly chopped
2 carrots, unpeeled, roughly
  chopped
3 celery sticks, roughly chopped
2 tomatoes, roughly chopped
  (optional)
1 tbsp tomato purée (optional)
cloves from ½ bulb of garlic,
  unpeeled
2 bay leaves
a few stems of any of the
  following – thyme, oregano,
  tarragon, basil, parsley
1 tsp peppercorns
100ml white wine (optional)

1. Heat the oil in a large saucepan. Add the onion and fry over a high heat until it starts to take on a bit of colour. Add the leeks, carrots and celery and continue to cook for another 5 minutes, stirring regularly.

2. Add the tomatoes and tomato purée, if using, then cook for another 2–3 minutes. Add the garlic, herbs and peppercorns, then pour in the wine, if using. Bring to the boil, then add 2 litres of water.

3. Bring to the boil, then reduce the heat until the stock is gently simmering. Simmer for about 1 hour, partially covered, then remove the pan from the heat and strain the stock. Leave to cool down. Store in the fridge for up to a week) or freeze – best used within 6 months.

ONE-POT

Onion Gravy

You can't have toad in the hole (see page 168) without lashings of onion gravy – my family's favourite.

Serves 6-8

500g onions, peeled (about 3 large)
25g butter
1 tbsp brown sugar
½ tsp dried thyme
1 tbsp plain flour
100ml red wine
750ml good-quality beef stock
1 tsp redcurrant or apple jelly (optional)
salt and black pepper

1. Cut the onions in half and slice them as finely as you can into half-moons.

2. Melt the butter in a large, lidded frying pan. Add the onions and cook them over a medium–low heat, stirring regularly, until the onions have collapsed and started to brown. This will probably take at least 30 minutes.

3. Stir in the sugar and thyme and season with plenty of salt and pepper. Turn up the heat and cook, still stirring regularly, for another 5 minutes. The onions should be very soft, brown and sticky.

4. Sprinkle over the flour and stir it into the onions, then pour in the red wine. It should bubble up and create a lot of steam. Stir really vigorously at this point – you want to make sure you scrape up all the sticky bits from the base of the pan.

5. Add all the stock and stir to combine, still making sure the base of the pan is clean. Bring to the boil, then turn down the heat and leave to simmer gently until you are ready to serve. Taste and adjust the seasoning. Add the redcurrant or apple jelly if you want the gravy slightly sweeter.

Croutons

These are a great way of using up stale bread and add a welcome bit of crunch to salads and soups.

Makes 200g

4 tbsp olive oil
1 garlic clove, crushed
1 tsp dried rosemary (optional)
200g thickly sliced bread, cut into cubes
salt

1. Preheat your oven to 200°C/180°C fan/gas 6. Put the oil, garlic and rosemary, if using, in a bowl and add a pinch of salt. Add the cubes of bread and toss until they are well coated.

2. Spread the cubes over a baking tray and bake in the oven for about 15 minutes. Keep checking and giving the tray a shake every few minutes until the croutons are crisp and golden brown. Remove and leave to cool. These keep really well in an airtight container for up to a week.

Spice Mix

Yes, you can buy loads of different spice mixes, but sometimes it's nice to make your own. I like this combination, so give it a try.

Makes 4 tablespoons

2 tsp each of cardamom seeds, coriander seeds and cumin seeds
1 tsp each of fennel seeds, fenugreek seeds and white pepper
8 cloves
4cm cinnamon stick
4 spokes from a star anise
2 bay leaves
½ tsp ground turmeric

1. Put all the whole spices and bay leaf into a dry frying pan and toast over a medium heat. Shake the pan regularly until the spices give off a strong aroma.

2. Remove from the heat and tip the spices onto a plate to cool down. Grind in a spice grinder or using a pestle and mortar, then stir in the ground turmeric. Store in an airtight jar.

Family life

♡

Stacey and me – we both hold the Jungle so close to our hearts. We look back now and think how mad that that was what brought us together. We'd both given up on the idea of having the perfect family life and then we found each other. Now we have two kids between us and three other beautiful children from different relationships who we love just as passionately. They all mean so much to us. We pinch ourselves sometimes when we think just how lucky we are, and we thank the Jungle and we thank fate. We have this amazing family, and we wouldn't change things for the world.

Life in our house is busy! We have five kids at different ages, ranging from a teenager to a baby, and they all need different things emotionally and physically. We are constantly on the go, keeping everyone entertained and happy. It's non-stop but we wouldn't change anything about our lives. I might go to work and be on stage in front of a few thousand people, then feel really good about myself afterwards, but for me, there is no greater feeling of achievement than when I've been with the kids all day. I've fed them, cared for them, run around the garden with them, made them laugh, got them to bed. And no matter how glamorous any showbiz event might be, that feeling after a day with the kids is the best in the world.

I always think that for Stacey and me every day chucks us a different challenge. We both work extremely hard on our careers, but the most important thing for us is that our family is happy. Every day is a juggling act, and we are so lucky that we have such amazing support from my mum, Stacey's mum and dad and other family members. We couldn't manage to do what we do workwise without them. There is a saying that it takes a village to raise a child and it's true in my experience.

Our kids are so lucky. They are surrounded by love and security, and we always encourage them to express themselves and not to be embarrassed and hold back on us. We have our ups and downs, but our house is full of love and laughter. There are always lots of people around and toys everywhere. And we love every minute of it.

And my little secret is that I'm storing up support for the future. When I'm old, I'll have five people ready to feed me and wipe my bum! Who could ask for more?

Life in our house is busy!

♡

We pinch ourselves sometimes when we think how lucky we are

♡

Proper Custard

QUICK

ONE-POT

My kids love a bit of custard with a pie or a crumble and I've found it's easy to make in a variety of flavours.

Makes 500ml

600ml whole milk
1 vanilla pod
4 egg yolks
25g white or golden caster sugar
2 tsp cornflour

1. Pour the milk into a saucepan. Cut a slit lengthways along one side of the vanilla pod and add it to the milk. Bring to just under the boil, then remove the pan from the heat and leave the vanilla flavour to infuse the milk.

2. Put the egg yolks, sugar and cornflour into a bowl. Whisk – by hand or with electric beaters – until the mixture looks pale yellow and foamy.

3. Remove the vanilla pod from the milk. Reheat the milk, again, to just under boiling point, and pour it into the bowl of egg mixture from a height, whisking constantly as you do so. Wash the saucepan and pour the custard into it.

4. Cook over a very gentle heat, stirring constantly until the custard thickens. You will find it doesn't do much to start with, then will thicken very quickly, so don't stop stirring!

5. If you aren't using the custard right away, cover with clingfilm, making sure it touches the custard. This stops a skin forming on the surface.

Joe's Tip

When you have used the vanilla pod, dry it thoroughly and use again. Or, you can put it in a jar of sugar to make vanilla sugar, which you can use in place of regular sugar in any cake so you don't have to add vanilla extract. Add to coffee to give a subtle vanilla kick or sprinkle over pancakes.

Variations

CHOCOLATE CUSTARD
Mix 25g cocoa with the cornflour and mix with the egg yolks and sugar as above.

PINK CUSTARD
Take 100g raspberries or strawberries. Put them in a pan with a splash of water and cook until just softened. Push through a sieve and add the liquid to the custard after all the other ingredients have been combined.

Index

Thank you all so much!

I've loved making this book and I want to thank all the amazing people who've helped make it happen.

Big thank you to Catherine Phipps and Jinny Johnson who worked with me on the recipes and ideas, and to editors Cara Armstrong and Vicky Orchard for their input and advice. Thanks to Nikki Dupin for the design and Dan Jones who took all the photos of the food and of me and my family. Saskia Sidey, Flossy McAslan and Natalie Thomson did a great job with the food styling and Megan Thomson with the props.

A special thanks to my manager Hannah Fletcher, the YMU management team Naomi Hodson and Martha Atack, and my literary team, Amanda and Elise – so appreciate all your support.

Lastly, I'd like to thank our five amazing children for being themselves – and enjoying my cooking – my sisters, Shana and Caisie Swash and, most of all, the three incredible women who've made me what I am – my mum, my nan Frannie and, of course, Stacey. I love you all more than I can say.

Pavilion
An imprint of HarperCollins*Publishers* Ltd
1 London Bridge Street
London SE1 9GF

www.harpercollins.co.uk

HarperCollins*Publishers*
1st Floor, Watermarque Building
Ringsend Road Dublin 4
Ireland

10 9 8 7 6 5 4 3 2 1

First published in Great Britain by
Pavilion, an imprint of HarperCollins*Publishers* Ltd 2022

ISBN 978-0-00-856072-0

This book is produced from independently certified FSC™ paper
to ensure responsible forest management.

For more information visit:
www.harpercollins.co.uk/green

Printed and bound in Italy

Executive Publisher: Lisa Milton
Publishing Director: Stephanie Milner
Commissioning Editor: Cara Armstrong
Managing Editor: Clare Double
Design Manager: Laura Russell
Photography: Dan Jones
Photography Assistants: Rosie Alsop, Zoe Warde-Aldam
Design and Art Direction: Nikki Dupin / Studio Nic & Lou
Additonal On-Set Art Direction: Bess Daley
Project Editor: Vicky Orchard
Food Stylists: Saskia Sidey, Flossy MacAslan, Natalie Thomson
Prop Stylist: Megan Thomson
Set Stylist: Andie Redman
Hair and Makeup: Penelope Smith and Tori Ball
Proofreader: Tamsin English
Indexer: Vanessa Bird

When using kitchen appliances please always follow the manufacturer's instructions.